SOCIAL CONSTRUCTION IN COUPLE AND FAMILY COUNSELING

Edited by
John D. West
Donald L. Bubenzer
James Robert Bitter

AMERICAN COUNSELING ASSOCIATION

THE FAMILY PSYCHOLOGY AND COUNSELING SERIES
Jon Carlson, Editor

SOCIAL CONSTRUCTION IN COUPLE AND FAMILY COUNSELING

American Counseling Association
5999 Stevenson Avenue
Alexandria, VA 22304

Director of Communications
Carolyn Baker

Director of Publishing Systems
Michael Comlish

Copyeditor
Marty Christy

Library of Congress Cataloging-in-Publication Data

West, John D.

Social construction in couple and family counseling/John D. West, James Robert Bitter, Donald L. Bubenzer.

p. cm. — (The Family psychology and counseling series)

Includes bibliographical references and index.

ISBN 1-55620-165-6 (alk. paper)

1. Family counseling. 2. Self-perception. 3. Psychotherapy—Methodology. 4. Counselors—Training of. I. Bitter, James Robert. II. Bubenzer, Don. III. Title. IV. Series.
HQ10.W39 1998
362.82'86—dc21

97-49144
CIP

The Family Psychology and Counseling Series

Counseling the Aging and Their Families
Irene Deitch, PhD, and Candace Ward Howell, MS

Counseling Families With Chronic Illness
Susan McDaniel, PhD

Mid-Life Divorce Counseling
Lita Linzer Schwartz, PhD

Social Construction in Couple and Family Counseling
John D. West, EdD, Donald L. Bubenzer, PhD and James Robert Bitter, EdD

Transitioning From Individual to Family Counseling
Charles Huber, PhD

Understanding Stepfamilies: Implications for Assessment and Treatment
Debra Huntley, PhD

In Preparation

Counseling Asian Families From a Systems Perspective
Kit S. Ng, PhD

Feminist Family Therapy
Kathleen May, PhD

Techniques in Couple and Family Therapy, Volume 1
Richard E. Watts, PhD

Techniques in Couple and Family Therapy, Volume 2
Richard E. Watts, PhD

Advisory Board

THE FAMILY PSYCHOLOGY AND COUNSELING SERIES

Table of Contents

From the Series Editor — vii
Jon Carlson, PsyD, EdD

Preface — ix
James Robert Bitter, EdD, John D. West, EdD, and Donald L. Bubenzer, PhD

Biographies — xvii

Contributors — xix

PART I. SOCIAL CONSTRUCTION THEORY

Chapter 1. Social Construction: A Family Perspective for the 21st Century — 3
Shelly Boughner, PhD, A. Spencer Davis, EdD, and Grace Ann Mims, PhD

PART II. SOCIAL CONSTRUCTION THEORY AND COUNSELING

Chapter 2. A Solution-Oriented Approach in Couple and Family Counseling — 21
John M. Littrell, EdD, and Jeffrey J. Angera, PhD

Chapter 3. A Narrative Perspective on Counseling With Couples and Families — 55
John D. West, EdD, Donald L. Bubenzer, PhD, Jacqueline A. Walsh, MS, and Hande Sensoy, MEd

Chapter 4. The Reflecting Position: Theoretical, Counselor, and Client Perspectives 79
John J. Zarski, PhD, Alan L. Sterling, MD, and Patricia E. Parr, PhD

Chapter 5. Family Counseling as Problem Dis-Solving and Collateral Learning: The Pragmatism of Harry Goolishian and G. Bob Gowin 101
Lyle J. White, PhD, and M. Harry Daniels, PhD

PART III. SOCIAL CONSTRUCTION THEORY AND COUNSELOR EDUCATION

Chapter 6. Tom Andersen's Comments on Reflecting Processes and Some Observations on Reflecting Practices in Supervision 123
Jane A. Cox, PhD, and Nadene A. L'Amoreaux, MA

Chapter 7. Discovering a Choice of Lenses: A Postmodern Approach to Couple and Family Counselor Training 135
Ellen S. Amatea, PhD, Peter A. D. Sherrard, EdD, and Silvia Echevarria Rafuls, PhD

PART IV. EPILOGUE

Chapter 8. Epilogue: Social Constructionism in the Evolution of Family Therapy 173
Karl Tomm, MD

From the Series Editor

> If you did nothing more when you have a family together than to make it possible for them to really look at each other, really touch each other, you would have already swung the pendulum in the direction of a new start. —Virginia Satir (1988)

Society seems to be changing from an objective perspective on facts to a more constructivist approach on meaning. According to Niemeyer (1995), Constructivism represents a stance that emphasizes self-conceiving, self-organizing, and proactive features of human knowing. The growing interest in the social construction of reality holds implications for the field of couple and family therapy. Therefore, ***Social Construction in Couple and Family Counseling*** was created to address this void.

The editors have chosen some outstanding thinkers and addressed some important issues. They readily acknowledge the multiple realities or perspectives that exist in this field and set the stage for a postmodern explanation. The importance of language and stories in determining reality is clearly explained. The authors also show how stories can and must be rewritten if healthy lives are to be created and lived. Furthermore, the need for new stories is tantamount if democratic living is to be created and oppression reduced.

The stories of the dominant culture must be rewritten if effective therapy is to occur. The data seem clear that the greatest number of couples and families who seek professional counseling will be poor and from non-White culture. The authors of these chapters show how therapists can be sensitized to their own prejudiced views in this regard. As Harlene Anderson (1997) states,

> The dominant voice, the culturally designated professional voice, usually speaks and decides for marginal population—gender, economic, ethnic, religious, political, and racial minorities—whether therapy is indicated and, if so, which therapy and toward what purpose. Sometimes unwittingly, sometimes knowingly, therapists subjugate or sacrifice a client to the influences of this broader context, which is primarily patriarchal, authoritarian, and hierarchical (p. xv)

The chapters of this important volume show how counselors can help couples and families to construct alternate understandings of their presenting concerns. Narrative, solution-focused, reflecting teams, and linguistic systems are highlighted.

I congratulate the contributors for providing the tools needed to learn how to construct alternative realities for the people whom we serve.

—Jon Carlson PsyD, EdD
Series Editor

References

Anderson, H. (1997). *Conversation, language, and possibilities.* New York: Basic Books.

Niemeyer, R. A. (1995). An appraisal of constructivist psychotherapies. In M. J. Mahoney (Ed.), *Cognitive and constructive psychotherapies: Theory, research and practice* (pp. 163–194). New York: Springer.

Satir, V. (1988). *The new peoplemaking.* Palo Alto, CA: Science and Behavior Books.

Preface

At the third Evolution of Psychotherapy Conference, held in Las Vegas in December 1995, Salvador Minuchin was asked why so many different approaches to therapy could still be effective. He answered that a therapist and client enter into a relationship in which they co-create a language for working together; to the extent that they are able to usefully employ this "new" language together, the foundation for effective change has been laid and is already possible (Minuchin, 1995). Minuchin's answer is gracious in many ways; it also acknowledges the multiple realities that have always constituted couple and family counseling.

When systems therapists created a paradigm shift in our understanding of human beings, a singular focus on the individual-in-isolation became the problem to overcome. In many ways, however, early systems theories merely enlarged the central unit of therapeutic focus; that is, the couple or family was now the focus of therapy as opposed to the individual. The belief that there were central truths and explanations for both functional and dysfunctional human systems remained. Bowen's (1976, 1978) multigenerational approach emphasized the power of systems to transmit rules and processes as well as problems over several generations, the need for differentiation, and the problems caused by triangulation. Satir focused on communication in assessment and intervention, using congruence, nurturance, connection, and validation to facilitate change (Satir, 1983; Satir & Bitter, 1997).

Though Whitaker was fond of claiming an atheoretical approach, he clearly felt that enlarging a family's capacity to experience was essential (Keith & Whitaker, 1991). And to varying degrees, Minuchin (1974) and the strategic therapists (Haley, 1976; Watzlawick, Weakland, & Fisch, 1974) believed that "structure" had to be assessed and addressed if therapists were to keep "problems" from defining, maintaining, and reifying systems. Each of these approaches is based on the belief that there is a truth to any system (expressed in processes, structures, rules, and interactions) that when identified will explain all human behavior within the system. This modernist perspective, still prominent in medicine, science, economics, and religion, has, until recently, permeated much of American family therapy.

Now, almost five decades into the systemic revolution, marriage and family counseling integrates information from multiple perspectives. There is a pragmatism to multiplicity; like William James and the squirrel (James, 1907) circling the same tree on opposites sides, different perspectives lead to different meanings and a different way of constructing knowledge. Indeed, had James been focused on the tree as opposed to the movement of the squirrel, his pluralistic beliefs (James, 1981) would have led him to a fuller experience of the object by touching it, standing back from it, climbing into it, and moving around it. In couple and family counseling, we seek to consider and ultimately know human systems from as many angles and as completely as possible. It is now common to be informed by gender; culture; socioeconomic position; history; politics and social policy; developmental issues and processes, often differentiated for boys and girls; and even spirituality. The impact of mental illness on the family is now as essential to our understanding of systems as the impact of system once was on our understanding of mental illness. We have entered the postmodern world where truth and "what is essential" are understood to be one of many conceptualizations or points of view, each bound by its own history and the contexts in which it emerged.

Multiple realities or perspectives exist in any field and in any human endeavor. Some of these realities, over time, gain more power than others. The French philosopher Michel Foucault (1970, 1980) called the various life perspectives we encounter "knowledge-positions." When one knowledge-position is infused with more power than others, it becomes dominant and is sometimes referred to as the truth. Dominant knowledge-positions are mostly maintained by claims to established and accepted practices, processes that generate and constitute proof of the dominant position. In a postmodern world, however, dominant knowledge-positions are merely more popular or widely accepted stories or narratives about life. Because dominant narratives focus on the maintenance of power, the processes that support these stories serve two functions: (a) to reinforce and maintain themselves and (b) to eliminate or minimize alternative stories and explanations.

In postmodern thought, language and the use of language in narrative leads to meaning. There is a unique meaning-narrative for each person who tells a story, and each story is always true for the person telling it. Two questions of significance to counselors are, How do these stories and perspectives come into being—what constitutes and maintains them? and Do the stories serve the system and the people in the system well?

When Peter Berger and Thomas Luckmann (1966) and later Kenneth Gergen (1985, 1991) and others emphasized the development of meaning in the context of social interaction, the field of social constructionism was born. Because we are inherently social creatures, we make meaning in relationship to other people, in conversation and dialogue. Even meaning we generate from reflection is often the result of an internal dialogue, in which we posit ourselves as both partners in a conversation.

When we are little or feel helpless, overwhelmed, and in need of support, dominant knowledge-positions and the stories attached to them tend to win out. "Dominant stories" (White & Epston, 1990, p. 41) often incorporate power positions and perspectives from larger systems (e.g., society, religion, or culture), and they appear to have the consensual validation of the larger number of others who exist in those systems.

To be sure, there is often some value in dominant positions and dominant stories. They may provide people and systems with much needed support for a while, perhaps a long while. A child may initially accept the dominant knowledge-position and story of the family and seek to find a place within that story; once the child feels a part of the story, there is a security experienced, often a sense of continuity and predictability that aids in one's coping with life. Eventually, the child will also contribute to the story's development, contradict it, attempt to shape it. The family story evolves into many stories. It is highly likely, however, that the family story that achieves dominance will be heavily informed by the larger systems of which it is a part. Society in general, culture, and community, all foster normative behavior in subsystems and seek to maintain dominance through conformity.

Foucault (1980) thought it was important to take a stand against all forms of dominant culture; he was engaged in an effort to maintain alternatives at all costs. Social constructionists may not fight dominant culture in all instances, but they hear a special call to action when a dominant story is no longer useful, when the story becomes "problem-saturated" (White & Epston, 1990, p. 16) and has eliminated needed alternatives, when the system and the people in it are stuck in a dysfunctional or useless story.

In the Greek world, *theoria* meant "seeing the sites," getting a worldview. According to Walter (1988), the world theorists who traveled exercised an integrated "seeing," and these wise ones used a complex mode of observation that included asking questions and listening to stories and myths. This observation encouraged an open receptivity to all kinds of phenomena. It was a holistic practice of thoughtful awareness. For us, social constructionist approaches to counseling are about helping folks to see the sites of their lives in some new ways. Social constructionist counseling is about locating experience in ways useful to people. It is about attaching positive or useful energy to the places of the memory, to the presentness of our lives and to our visions for the future. Social constructionist approaches offer collaboration with couples and families to provide the agency for them to construct, maintain, and extend themselves in ways to which they are committed.

In recent years, many articles and books have broadened the appeal of social constructionism. Two books in particular have helped to delineate postmodern approaches to therapeutic processes. *Therapy As Social Construction* (McNamee & Gergen, 1992) addressed theoretical contexts, therapeutic practice, and issues raised from reflective consideration. In it, Karl Tomm, Tom Andersen, Lynn Hoffman, Harlene Anderson and Harold Goolishian, William O'Hanlon, and David Epston and Michael White, to name a few, used examples and fully developed case studies to bring therapy as social construction to life. *Therapeutic Conversations* (Gilligan & Price, 1993) took the dialogue of social constructionists to a new level. Based on a conference originally conceived by Bill O'Hanlon and Reese Price and held in Tulsa, Oklahoma, in June 1992, the book presented positions and commentaries by many of the people who had initiated the dialogue and were influencing the paradigm shift, including Karl Tomm, John Weakland, Steve de Shazer, William O'Hanlon, Michele Weiner-Davis, David Epston, and Michael White. Although social constructionism is not distinctly applied to couples and families, *Therapeutic Conversations* was one of the first books to devote substantive material to these systemic units. This present effort, *Social Construction in Couple and Family Counseling*, considers social construction theory and its relevance to counselors and counselor educators as they work with couples, families, and students in counselor education programs.

The text is divided into eight chapters with the first chapter by Shelly Boughner, A. Spencer Davis, and Grace Ann Mims taking a historical perspective on social construction theory. They note that we create our understandings and beliefs through the interactions we have with others and that these interactions are based in languaging or discourse. The authors indicate that in social construction theory the counselor works collaboratively with clients in constructing alternative understandings about their presenting concerns. The remaining chapters amplify Chapter 1 by discussing the manifestations of social constructionist ideas in more specific therapeutic, supervisory, and educational practices.

In Chapter 2, John M. Littrell and Jeffrey J. Angera present thoughts on a solution-oriented approach to counseling with couples and families. They do this by describing Angera's work with a family that lasted over a nine-month period. The authors have a dialogue about the solution-oriented work that occurred with this family, and they present for consideration other solution-oriented questions that were not asked in the case but are in keeping with their approach to counseling. In Chapter 3, John D. West, Donald L. Bubenzer, Jacqueline A. Walsh, and Hande Sensoy describe a narrative approach to counseling with families and couples. They note that the narrative approach is interested in the multiple stories that are embedded in relationships, and they refer to literature that provides a description of the impact of these stories in one's life. They also describe the counseling process as collaborative, where clients are helped to question the assumption that their relationship is exclusively comprised of one story and where clients are helped to identify stories about relationships that contain valued outcomes. In Chapter 4, John J. Zarski, Alan L. Sterling, and Patricia E. Parr present a theoretical basis for considering the use of reflecting teams in counseling with couples and families. They also discuss the role of a counselor in the reflecting position and note that the role is one of being collaborative and consultative rather than being a privileged expert. The authors go on to note that reflecting teams seem helpful when they are able to bring to the surface multiple perspectives for clients who are experiencing a therapeutic impasse. In Chapter 5, Lyle J. White and M. Harry Daniels present an integration of the ideas of two social constructionists, Harry Goolishian and G. Bob Gowin, and they offer thoughts on how their work contributes to couple and family counseling. They propose that by entering the clients' linguistic systems as a collateral learner, the counselor can help facilitate change in clients' lives. In part, facilitating this change is thought to occur during conversations that are oriented toward defining the clients' presenting problem. During these conversations the counselor works in an effort to ensure that all voices are heard, and it is thought that as perspectives are broadened and new meanings are constructed, a dis-solving of presenting problems may occur.

Jane A. Cox and Nadene A. L'Amoreaux, in Chapter 6, consider the use of reflecting teams in counselor supervision. Portions of this chapter include an interview with Tom Andersen, in which he discusses premises that are important to his work. In Chapter 7, Ellen S. Amatea, Peter A. D. Sherrard, and Silvia Echevarria Rafuls have taken time to consider some postmodern ways of thinking, and they have attempted to differentiate epistemological lenses through which to view families. The authors discuss ways these lenses are introduced to students in their counselor education program at the University of Florida. Karl Tomm, in Chapter 8, offers his personal view regarding changes in family therapy over the past 30 years. These changes include movement from viewing individuals to viewing systems, movement from seeing systems as interacting to seeing systems as observing and making meaning, and now from this observing systems approach to seeing the political effects of certain patterns of seeing, that is, making meaning. Finally, Tomm discusses ethical issues related to the selection of meanings or constructs in the light of the impact of such meaning making.

James Robert Bitter, EdD
John D. West, EdD
Donald L. Bubenzer, PhD
Editors

References

Berger, P., & Luckmann, T. (1966). *The social construction of reality.* Garden City, NY: Doubleday.

Bowen, M. (1976). Theory in the practice of psychotherapy. In P. J. Guerin, Jr. (Ed.), *Family therapy: Theory and practice* (pp. 42–90). New York: Gardner Press.

Bowen, M. (1978). *Family therapy in clinical practice.* New York: Aronson.

Foucault, M. (1970). *The order of things: An archaeology of the human sciences.* New York: Random House.

Foucault, M. (1980). *Power/knowledge: Selected interviews and other writings.* New York: Pantheon Books.

Gergen, K. (1985). The social constructionist movement in modern psychology. *American Psychologist, 40,* 266–275.

Gergen, K. (1991). *The saturated self.* New York: Basic Books.

Gilligan, S., & Price, R. (Eds.). (1993). *Therapeutic conversations.* New York: Norton.

Haley, J. (1976). *Problem-solving therapy: New strategies for effective family therapy.* San Francisco: Jossey-Bass.

James, W. (1907). *Pragmatism: A new name for some old ways of thinking.* New York: Longmans, Green.

James, W. (1981). *The works of William James: The principles of psychology* (Vols. I–III). Cambridge, MA: Harvard University Press.

Keith, D. V., & Whitaker, C. A. (1991). Experiential/symbolic family therapy. In A. M. Horne & J. L. Passmore (Eds.), *Family counseling and therapy* (2nd ed., pp. 107–140). Itasca, IL: F. E. Peacock.

McNamee, S., & Gergen, K. J. (Eds.). (1992). *Therapy as social construction.* Newbury Park, CA: Sage.

Minuchin, S. (1974). *Families and family therapy.* Cambridge, MA: Harvard University Press.

Minuchin, S. (Speaker). (1995). *Conversation hour: Third conference on the evolution of psychotherapy* (Cassette Recording No. MH260-CH9). Huntington Beach, CA: Sound Waves Production.

Satir, V. M. (1983). *Conjoint family therapy* (3rd. ed.). Palo Alto, CA: Science and Behavior Books.

Satir, V. M., & Bitter, J. R. (1997). The therapist and family therapy: Satir's human validation process model. In A. M. Horne & J. L. Passmore (Eds.), *Family counseling and therapy* (3rd ed.). Itasca, IL: F. E. Peacock.

Walter, E. V. (1988). *Placeways: A theory of the human environment.* Chapel Hill, NC: University of North Carolina Press.

Watzlawick, P., Weakland, J. H., & Fisch, R. (1974). *Change: Principles of problem formation and problem resolution.* New York: Norton.

White, M., & Epston, D. (1990). *Narrative means to therapeutic ends.* New York: Norton.

Biographies

John D. West, EdD, is a Professor in the Counseling and Human Development Services (CHDS) Program at Kent State University and coordinator of doctoral preparation in the CHDS Doctoral Program (a CACREP-accredited Counselor Education and Supervision doctoral program). For over 20 years he, along with others, has published manuscripts on a number of issues including topics related to family counseling and counselor education. At present he enjoys considering the place of social construction theory in counselor preparation as well as in other aspects of life. John and his wife, Eileen, are parents of two daughters, Erin and Anne.

Donald L. Bubenzer, PhD, is a Professor in the Counseling and Human Development Services Program and Chair of the Adult, Counseling, Health, and Vocational Education Department at Kent State University. He regularly teaches courses in couple and family counseling and along with John West authored the book *Counselling Couples*. Together with John West, he has interviewed numerous internationally known social constructionist family therapists. These interviews have been published in *The Family Journal: Counseling and Therapy for Couples and Families*. In addition to his professional pursuits, Don is interested in the relationship of our social constructs of the natural world and our stewardship of and intentions within that world. Don and Nancy, a school counselor, are the parents of two daughters, Amy and Stacey.

James Robert Bitter, EdD, is a Professor of Counseling and Chair of Human Development and Learning at East Tennessee State University. He teaches courses in couple and family counseling, and he is editor of *Individual Psychology: The Journal of Adlerian Theory, Research, and Practice.* Jim worked for 10 years with the late pioneer of family therapy, Virginia Satir, and together they coauthored a number of articles and chapters. At present, he is using narrative therapy and social construction theory to bridge the work of individual therapy and family systems therapy. He also is engaged in bringing a social construction process to a consideration of personal and professional ethics. Jim and his wife, Lynn Williams, have a five-year-old daughter, Alison Harper Williams.

Jon Carlson, PsyD, EdD, is Distinguished Professor at Governors State University in University Park, Illinois, and Director of the Lake Geneva Wellness Clinic in Wisconsin. He is the editor of *The Family Journal: Counseling and Therapy for Couples and Families* and has served as president of the International Association of Marriage and Family Counselors.

Contributors

Ellen S. Amatea, PhD, is a Professor in the Department of Counselor Education, University of Florida, Gainesville, Florida.

Jeffrey J. Angera, PhD, is a Counselor in the Counseling Center and Adjunct Assistant Professor in the Department of Human Environmental Studies, Central Michigan University, Mt. Pleasant, Michigan.

James Robert Bitter, EdD, is a Professor of Counseling and Chair of Human Development and Learning, East Tennessee State University, Johnson City, Tennessee.

Shelly Boughner, PhD, is an Assistant Professor in the Division of Educational Psychology and Counseling, University of South Dakota, Vermillion, South Dakota.

Donald L. Bubenzer, PhD, is a Professor in the Counseling and Human Development Services Program and Chair in the Department of Adult, Counseling, Health, and Vocational Education, Kent State University, Kent, Ohio.

Jane A. Cox, PhD, is an Assistant Professor in the Department of Educational Psychology and Special Education, Southern Illinois University at Carbondale, Carbondale, Illinois.

M. Harry Daniels, PhD, is a Professor and Chair in the Department of Counselor Education, University of Florida, Gainesville, Florida.

A. Spencer Davis, EdD, is a Counselor in private practice at the Rocky Mountain Clinic in Butte, Montana.

Nadene A. L'Amoreaux, MA, is a doctoral student in the Counseling and Human Development Services Program, Kent State University, Kent, Ohio.

John M. Littrell, EdD, is a Professor in the Department of Professional Studies in Education, Counselor Education, Iowa State University, Ames, Iowa.

Grace Ann Mims, PhD, is an Assistant Professor in the Division of Educational Psychology and Counseling, University of South Dakota, Vermillion, South Dakota.

Patricia E. Parr, PhD, is an Assistant Professor in the Marriage and Family Therapy Training Program, The University of Akron, Akron, Ohio.

Silvia Echevarria Rafuls, PhD, is an Assistant Professor in the Department of Counselor Education, University of Florida, Gainesville, Florida.

Hande Sensoy, MEd, is a doctoral student in the Counseling and Human Development Services Program, Kent State University, Kent, Ohio.

Peter A. D. Sherrard, EdD, is an Associate Professor in the Department of Counselor Education, University of Florida, Gainesville, Florida.

Alan L. Sterling, MD, is the Medical Director at the Akron Child Guidance Center and a part-time faculty member at The University of Akron, Akron, Ohio.

Karl Tomm, MD, is a Professor and Director of the Family Therapy Program in the Department of Psychiatry, Faculty of Medicine, The University of Calgary, Calgary, Alberta.

Jacqueline A. Walsh, MS, is a doctoral student in the Counseling and Human Development Services Program, Kent State University, Kent, Ohio.

John D. West, EdD, is a Professor in the Counseling and Human Development Services Program, Kent State University, Kent, Ohio.

Lyle J. White, PhD, is an Associate Professor in the Department of Educational Psychology and Special Education, Southern Illinois University at Carbondale, Carbondale, Illinois.

John J. Zarski, PhD, is a Professor in the Marriage and Family Therapy Training Program, The University of Akron, Akron, Ohio.

PART I

SOCIAL CONSTRUCTION THEORY

FROM: SOCIAL CONSTRUCTION IN COUPLE & FAMILY COUSELLING. (1998).

1

Social Construction: A Family Perspective for the 21st Century

Shelly Boughner, PhD
A. Spencer Davis, EdD
Grace Ann Mims, PhD

In this chapter we consider the relevance of social construction theory for couple and family counseling. We have provided a brief historical perspective and examples that illustrate the usefulness of social construction theory for counselors.

Social Construction in a Postmodern World

Social construction theories highlight the social origins of our taken-for-granted assumptions about reality. Gergen (1985) stated that these theories "direct our attention to the social, moral, political, and economic institutions that sustain and are supported by current assumptions about human activity" (pp. 267–268). The notion that currently prevailing views may be no more correct or natural than views residing at the margins raises issues of diversity and cultural variability. Social construction invites inquiry into the historical and cultural foundations of our views of reality, and the ways of life that these afford.

Social construction theories appear to be gaining attention in part just now because of their compatibility with the current emphasis on the intellectual movements of postmodernism and multiculturalism. Norris (1990) defined a postmodern attitude as one of "thoroughgoing skeptical doubt in regard to questions of truth, meaning, and historical interpretation" (p. 29). Postmodernism is a reaction to the modern worldview that sought to establish reason as the prime mover (Tarnas, 1991). In modern approaches to knowledge, classificatory systems were used. The classification of plants into categories such as genus or species is an example of this classificatory approach. When applied to objects of knowledge within the human realm (e.g., ideas, values, beliefs, identities, etc.), this approach to knowledge was less useful although just as industriously applied. Postmodern approaches to knowledge challenge this classification method and provide alternative routes to knowledge. Within a postmodern approach, human or social realities are seen to escape the bounds of their categories and to resist a final, once and for all "knowing."

A hallmark of postmodern views is the inability to take for granted our assumptions about how reality stacks up. As traditional notions of truth are set aside, the ability to unambiguously align ourselves with "the right" and "the good" is surrendered. A vision has been called forth that acknowledges the pluralism, complexity, and ambiguity of the contemporary intellectual scene. Virtually every important element of the Western intellectual past is now present and active in one form or another, contributing to the vitality and confusion of the current historical moment.

The postmodern milieu has been marked by a burgeoning of perspectives in all areas of life. Traditional norms have been questioned and alternatives celebrated. Multiplicity has replaced convention in areas such as art, literature, architecture, philosophy, politics, and social discourse. In *The Saturated Self*, Gergen (1991) described the impact on everyday life of the cultural shift to postmodern perspectives along with the technological revolution of the late 20th century. People, according to Gergen, participate in multiple realities on a daily basis. People engage in multiple contexts with their multiple demands. Information from all parts of the world is immediately accessible. Perspectives, opinions, and theories, which may or may not conflict, form part of every interaction or experience. People negotiate these multiple contexts daily and manage to maintain some sense of coherence or continuity.

Although the postmodern era is without a universal truth regarding the nature of reality, it is rich with an unprecedented diversity of perspectives from which to confront the important issues that face humanity (Tarnas, 1991). It is at this point that social construction theories and postmodernism intersect. Both consider the pluralism of truth, strive to overcome the limitations imposed by traditional structures and foundations, provide a voice to marginalized groups and individuals, and promote an ideological commitment to legitimizing differences. Social construction may be defined as a variant of postmodern thought that emphasizes the primacy of *social* rather than *personal* constructions of reality (Lyddon, 1995).

Social Construction Theory

Social construction theories are among those versions of postmodern thought that seriously consider *self* and *reality* as lived out in everyday experience. Social construction theories propose that individuals are profoundly immersed in the social, that our understandings of and beliefs about ourselves and the world are social products. The self can only exist for itself, if it is recognized by others of consequence. Shotter (1989) stated that "in being addressed as a particular 'you,' in certain particular settings, by certain particular people, you come to know yourself as a particular kind of person among other such persons" (p. 148). A social construction account argues that the notion of an individual exterior to the social is an abstract formulation that is not borne out in the reality of our day to day lives. McGowan (1991) stated that "the unconstrained individual never existed anywhere" (p. 216). Selves are products of social processes. We are born into and live within social settings, as members of particular social groups. Our identities are shaped over time through intersubjective experiences. Recognition by others as a particular sort of person is a necessary part of identity formation.

Similarly, social construction theories suggest that the very terms in which we understand the world are "social artifacts, products of historically situated interchanges among people" (Gergen, 1985, p. 267). Understanding, in this view, results from the active, cooperative, interaction of persons in relationship. Understanding is grounded in discourse (language) and is irreducibly interactive. Schweder and Miller (1985) argued that "people categorize the world the way they do because they have participated in social practices, institutions, and other forms of symbolic action (e.g., language) that presuppose or in some way make salient those categorizations" (p. 41). The constructions (categories) may be many and varied, depending on the social contexts within which they arise, but in all cases they are in some sense tradition-bound and are shared through language. Simply stated, we create our understandings of ourselves and of the world through discourse with others in our own particular contexts.

An Illustration of the Social Construction of Identity

Social construction theories suggest, then, that we are situated in very particular ways, and that who we are and what we know is very much a result of the relationships in which we participate. We are, in a very real sense, who others know us to be. A useful illustration of the elemental role played by others in the constitution of a self is provided in the novel (1971) and film (1979) *Being There*, both written by Jerzy Kosinski. Peter Sellers starred in this film as Chance, an intellectually challenged gardener, who, by the end of the film, has been transformed into Chauncey Gardiner, a presidential advisor and potential candidate for high-level public office. This transformation takes place as a result of Chance's interactions with others, which produce meanings, (unintended by Chance) that profoundly alter his life and his self as known by others.

Chance spends his entire life within the confines of the house and garden in which he lives and works. The "Old Man" (whose death takes place at the beginning of the film), has provided Chance with food, lodging, and his own castoff clothing which consists of hand tailored suits from the 1920s. He has also forbidden Chance to leave the premises. At the point in time when the Old Man dies, Chance has experienced few interactions with other people. He and the Old Man have talked occasionally. He has interacted with the housekeeper, Louise, who has fixed his meals, and as a child was taught to garden by a man, Joe, who repaired the wall in the garden and spoke with Chance about various aspects of life. Chance spent most of his time watching television. The Old Man had provided television sets in every room and even in the garden. Because of the paucity of his experience with others, most of Chance's knowledge about people and the world came from television.

We are given to understand that Chance's life has been set up in this manner in response to his limited intellectual abilities. Louise's remark that he "will always be a child" seems an accurate assessment. Chance, a middle-aged man in the film, appears sweet, open, and trusting; he seems asexual, and without guile or pretense. Following the Old Man's death, Chance is asked to leave his home, and he ventures out into the city of Washington, D.C. Following a minor accident, in which Chance's leg is pinned between the bumper of a limousine and that of another car, he winds up staying in the home of a wealthy financier and his wife. At this point, through his interactions with these individuals and through them, and with other powerful and influential figures, Chance's transformation to Chauncey Gardiner takes place.

Eve, the wife of the financial magnate, mis-hears Chance as he introduces himself (following his mishap with her limousine), and when she subsequently refers to him as "Chauncey Gardiner," he responds. Those who interact with Chance, from the household staff to the president of the United States and talk show hosts, continue to mis-hear him and to understand his direct, concrete speech as implying other metaphorical meanings. He speaks of gardening—all he knows—and those with whom he converses hear it as a metaphor regarding current financial trends. Ben Rand, the financier, remarks, "Yes, Chauncey, what an excellent metaphor! A productive businessman is indeed a laborer in his own vineyard!" (p. 34). Others take Chance to be "natural," a "truly peaceful man," to have a sense of humor, to be "very intense," and to be "brilliant" and "sexy." Their expectations, based on his finely tailored appearance, lead them to conclude that his meaning must be other than it appears on the surface. They hear, in effect, what they expect to hear.

Chance tells one man that he does not read nor write. The man responds, "Of course not. Who has time anymore?" When Eve makes sexual advances to Chance and he fails to respond, she asks him what is wrong. He states that he "likes to watch," meaning television, and she assumes that he is speaking in sexual terms. Chance is invited by Ben, the financier, to sit in on a meeting with the president of the United States. The president and Ben discuss the financial status of the country. When Chance is asked his opinion on these matters, he again speaks about the garden:

> In a garden growth has its season. There are spring and summer, but there are fall and winter. And then spring and summer again. As long as the roots are not severed, all is well and all will be well. (p. 45)

The president takes Chance's meaning to be metaphorical and responds by noting how refreshing and optimistic his comments are, and he elaborates on the metaphor, linking economic systems to natural cycles: "We welcome the inevitable seasons of nature, yet we are upset by the seasons of our economy! How foolish of us!" (p. 45). He goes on to remark that "I envy Mr. Gardiner his good solid sense. This is just what we lack on Capitol Hill" (p. 45).

Part of Chance's propensity to be mis-heard or misinterpreted arises from his affinity for watching television. At the time of the events related in the novel and film, Chance has spent much of nearly every day of his life watching television. He responds to events and people as he has seen others do on TV. He shakes hands in a two-handed manner when he meets the president and looks him directly in the eye, because that is how he has seen people behave on television when meeting the president. He often remarks, "I understand," or "I see," in conversation because television personalities converse in this way. Chance also repeats parts of others' sentences back to them, another conversational practice picked up from TV. Because Chance responds in this manner, those with whom he interacts continue speaking and elaborate on what they have said. They attribute to Chance qualities of comprehension and caring, and take themselves to be bright and interesting in his presence.

By the end of the film, Chance has been asked by Ben, to continue looking after his wife once Ben has died and to serve on the board of his multimillion dollar corporation. Chance's name is being considered as a potential candidate for president or vice president, and Chance has become a much-admired public figure. This simple gardener has become a major player in Washington's social, political, and economic circles. As readers and viewers we are aware that Chance has been made out to be someone he is not. The participants in the narrative, however, have only their experience to go by. They are acquainted with "Chauncey Gardiner" and interact with him accordingly. Chauncey is socially constructed in the extreme, and we are permitted to observe this process. Given that Chauncey's situation is both radical and unlikely to take place in any of our everyday lives, we turn now to the consideration of the social construction process in our day to day experience.

Social Construction in Everyday Life

The time in our lives when our experience most closely parallels that of Chance is childhood. As children, we participate in a range of social contexts that require certain actions on our part. We learn the norms or expectations of the groups to which we belong. At times, portions of our identities are constructed by these groups, with little or no input from us. Children do not, for the most part, announce to their significant others that they are "gifted," "learning disabled," or "artistically inclined." Others make those (and other) determinations and present them in various ways to the child. Parents, teachers, and other members of the child's community contribute to the child's identity, based on their interactions with and observations of the child. Children have little recourse to challenge these constructions, and for the most part they simply take them on and live them out. Regarding the power of this process of childhood socialization, Berger and Luckmann (1966) remarked that "He *is* what he is supposed to be, to himself as to his significant others and to the community as a whole" (p. 165).

The immediacy and concreteness of childhood constructions of meaning and identity may be recalled through the following examples. The reality presented on television or in the theater is often, for children, a matter of pure experience unmediated by objective analysis or by the notion that it is simply a story and is not really taking place. The death of Bambi's mother is cause for sorrow and tears, and the Wicked Witch of the West is best observed from behind the largest chair in the room. Meaning is taken up in absolute and total form as a product of immersion in the reality as presented. For children, it is not a matter of thinking, "Isn't it sad that she died," or "The witch is really pretty ruthless." Rather, the impact is emotional and remains unmediated by the distance of thought or reflection. It is, in Berger and Luckmann's (1966) terms, in the "here and now" (p. 22).

A similar approach is used by children in meeting situations that arise in everyday life. The following example was provided by a friend of the authors:

> One time, in first grade, there was a play put on at Brownies. It was really funny and I laughed so hard that I peed in my pants. One of the other girls blackmailed me about that for five years. She could get me to do anything she wanted by threatening to tell the other kids that I had this accident at Brownies. It wasn't until I was in fifth grade that I knew enough to just tell her to go ahead, and then she stopped bothering me.

The meaning of this situation for the child was immediate and emotionally driven. Childhood experiences are often characterized by this power and immediacy. When other children say that they "aren't our friend anymore" or we are left out of the "A" reading group, we interpret those events emotionally and in a literal manner. Our notions of self as children arise from events such as these. We become who others tell us we are.

As adults, we have greater latitude in contesting constructions that seem inappropriate or dissatisfying. Adults may challenge others' constructions through discourse and interaction. Alternative constructions may be suggested or the inappropriateness of certain constructions demonstrated. Because of the profoundly social nature of our experience, however, individual proposals of identity constructions may not always prevail. Others must acknowledge our identities and must interact with us in terms of those identities if the identities are to be maintained. This necessary involvement of others may be viewed in various contexts.

A hypothetical newly established couple may serve as an illustration of social construction in everyday life. The tasks faced by a new couple in establishing themselves as a couple and in negotiating the particulars of their joint identity are myriad. The expectations of the larger society regarding couples and criteria for inclusion in this class of relationships figure prominently. Questions that arise may include, How long have the two individuals been together? In what capacity? How permanent is the partnership? Have they formalized the arrangement in any way? The ability to receive recognition as a couple from various groups within society arises from responses to questions such as these. Although societal criteria have shifted regarding the classes of relationships that may constitute a recognized couple, particular groups within the society may use standards that are more or less restrictive. A couple within a college milieu may not be equivalent to a couple as recognized by a church or family group. Any particular couple must contend with the specific groups making up its context.

The identity of the couple is socially constructed from within the relationship as well. The partners each contribute to their joint identity and participate in ongoing negotiations in the construction of this identity. For example, the couple considers questions such as, What sort of people are we? How do we work out problems? What do we believe in or stand for? Who leads in what areas? What do we want for our future? Such aspects of a relationship are worked out through both verbal and nonverbal interaction, are both explicit and implicit, and continue to evolve over time. Once mutually satisfactory definitions are arrived at, they must be further negotiated with the wider social contexts in which the couple holds membership. If, for example, the couple arrives at an agreement regarding problem solving that allows physically aggressive persuasion, the wider social context may step in to challenge this internally acceptable definition.

The meaning of the partners' actions, verbalizations, and experiences is constantly worked out, revised, and clarified. If one partner hugs a member of the opposite sex, what does that mean about and for the couple? If one partner describes the other as "a saint," what does it mean? Is this a positive description? Is it more about the speaker's "wildness" than about the other's "goodness?" What does the statement imply about patterns of interaction? The negotiation of small discrete meanings is ongoing, as is the negotiation of larger more pervasive definitions. Identity formation is always in process and is always profoundly social.

Twelve-step programs provide an apt example of the importance of others in negotiating changes in identity. These programs provide individuals with a strongly influential social context or community that supports a new or altered identity during the transition from "how I was" to "how I am now." Friends, family members, and acquaintances who have shared history with the individual supporting the "old" identity often hesitate to endorse the new construction until they have acquired adequate experience with the individual that ratifies the changes. Other participants in the program provide immediate and sustained support of the new construction and actively assist in its maintenance. Often fellow participants become central figures in the lives of persons who take part in 12-step programs. They both recognize and respond to the nascent identity, take it seriously, and participate in its development.

At times, the social contexts in which one participates are less than supportive of changes in identity or of particular identity projects. In many cases, cultural notions about the kind of person one must be to receive validation or recognition are taken up by the entire range of social contexts in which individuals participate. If an individual attempts to be otherwise, his or her attempts may be challenged by others or he or she may risk losing recognition within significant social contexts. One example of this nonrecognition process in the current American cultural scene involves persons identified as being overweight. Cultural ideals for weight and appearance permeate nearly all social contexts. It would be difficult to locate portions of society that fail to endorse some version of "thin is better." The range of values attached to this notion of "better" is quite extensive. Definitions of "better" in various contexts may include healthier, more attractive, more energetic, more emotionally stable, more morally upright, and so forth. Persons who fail to correspond to this body type ideal often accrue identity descriptions that amount to being "worse" in various ways (e.g., they are lazy, have emotional problems, etc.). Often, even if a person comes to accept his or her own weight in spite of this ideal image, the failure of others to endorse the acceptability of being overweight can wreak havoc with identity projects that do not conform to the cultural ideal.

Social Construction in Couple and Family Counseling

If we accept the notion that reality is socially constructed—that what we understand and what we live out involves the participation of others in our various contexts—we may wonder what implications this view holds for various endeavors, among them, couples and family counseling. Social constructionism offers an avenue to meet the extraordinary challenges facing couples and families through a new commitment to the open exchange of many perspectives.

What is family? Is there a right way to be a family? How do we solve our problems? Who do we listen to? What are our values now? These and many others are the questions that confront the family counselor today. Definitions of family life are no longer static; that is, movement and change occur in many directions and everywhere. Our explanations and interventions for families have not necessarily kept pace with the rapid shifts in family life. Social construction theory sheds a different light on the issues of family treatment and allows for a range of answers to many of today's most difficult questions. The well-worn dogmas of the past are no longer sufficient for the present or future. What follows is our narrative of the place of social construction theory in the field of couple and family counseling.

The field of couple and family counseling has experienced major jumps over the past 40 years. Probably the greatest leap for family counseling came through the work of the early systemic thinkers: Watzlawick, Weakland, Fisch, Haley, Bateson, Jackson, Satir, Bowen, Minuchin, and others. (Bateson, 1971; Bateson, Jackson, Haley, & Weakland, 1956; Bertalanffy, 1968; Bowen, 1978; Haley, 1963; Jackson, 1967; Minuchin, 1974; Satir, 1964; Watzlawick, Beavin, & Jackson, 1967; Watzlawick, Weakland, & Fisch, 1974; Watzlawick & Weakland, 1977). These early family pioneers took the locus of pathology (problems) out of the individual and situated it in interactions between couples and family members. Problems were generated through the faulty interaction and communication patterns found in families. Individuals were no longer seen as being the locus of the problem, and hence the focus of intervention shifted as well. Interventions quickly spread to encompass the entire system of the family or the couple. Frequently, problems observed in children were deemed a by-product of a problematic couple's dyadic relationship. Interventions were thus focused on the sequences of interaction and communication. This shift in thinking, from the individual to the system, represents what may be the greatest leap in the treatment of family problems.

The social sciences have struggled to live up to their name. The past decades have seen theorists looking in vain for the truths that would define family life and transform the therapeutic process into a hard science. With near religious zeal, counselors, psychologists, and other therapists have embarked on the quest to learn and discover the answers to human dilemmas. Since B. F. Skinner (1953, 1971) first articulated the notion that the aim of psychology is the prediction and control of behavior, many people have been engaged in a never-ending search for an objective reality. Where has this search left us? Do we have a future as a science, or will we go the way of psychics? Perhaps our quest for truth and objective reality has not been for naught; at the very least we have arrived at the juncture of the modernist–postmodernist debate. History most likely will again repeat itself, and we will move forward with greater understanding. The future could never happen without the past.

Social construction theory presents a workable alternative to the search for truth. Once one accepts the notion that no final, absolute truth exists, at least in social relationships, acceptance of the subjective nature of human existence comes within reach. Family life is a tapestry of intertwined stories; all of these stories need to be told, understood, and accepted as legitimate. Families must know that their story is valued and accepted as a valid construction of and for their very existence. Who out there can actually decide the right way to be as a family? Though we do live in a society that says there are some ways a family cannot be (e.g., abusive), each of us has our own answer, and we try to find someone, anyone, who will share our story with us. A strong postmodern assumption is that there are multiple realities and points of view, and this may be the most facilitative starting point with any family.

Social construction theory breathes fresh air into couple and family counseling, giving us at the very least permission to be nonexperts. This has allowed family counselors to recognize that their construction of reality is merely their own point of view. This whole notion explodes the myth that a theory is anything but the theorist's personal construction or view of family life. In this sense then, every theory has status similar to a myth. We must recognize that many of these myths have been accepted as "the way it really is," or as Grand Narratives. Once an adequate number of people operate from a myth as if it were true, the myth or theory takes on sufficient power to convert people to its constructs. This leads to a following and counselors and others act as though the theory has solid foundation in objective reality. At this point, the theory generates practice.

In no way are we operating from a position which holds that theories are no longer useful. As we previously stated, the future cannot exist without the past. Without the work (creative brilliance) generated by those before us, we would not have been able to arrive at our present position. The major aim of social construction theory is to embrace alternative views, and at the same time to reflexively evaluate our own position.

Social construction theory is a great aid in understanding not only family life but also the life of the family (i.e., their interactions with the community, schools, churches, governments, cultures, races, etc.). This whole movement is really concerned with how people make meaning in their lives, how they construct reality. As a result, this represents a shift away from doing something therapeutic to the client family to doing something therapeutic with them. We, as professional helpers, do not possess the answer; instead, we believe that clients possess an answer but are unable to locate it in a form that is recognizable and useful. The idea then is for clients and counselors to work together to discover a way of being that the client judges to be preferred and to then find ways to act on this new understanding (Bubenzer, West, & Boughner, 1994).

Counseling, according to social construction theory, attempts to create an atmosphere of warmth and mutuality. The counselor's sense of mutuality and concern for co-creating a future with the client facilitiates a milieu in which the whole group (family plus counselor) becomes able to generate creative and flexible constructions. New stories that are produced may contain both useful descriptions of the family as well as alternative stories about the dilemmas that face the family. Lynn Hoffman (1988) summarized this type of therapeutic effort as follows:

> It avoids the implication of fixing something that has been broken down or is not functioning and comes closer to being some kind of hopeful discourse. It is, as far as possible, nonjudgmental, and nonperjorative. It is not control-oriented. It is lateral rather than hierarchical in structure. It is wary of an instructive stance. It shrinks away from an influence that is primarily intentional. It is pluralistic in nature, focusing on many views rather than one. There is no assumption of objectivity or truth. (p. 126)

As Hoffman pointed out, this style of counseling allows a more equal and shared responsibility for the counseling process. It is respectful and accepts that the family is really its own best expert, but is experiencing a period of relative inflexibility and stuckness. The therapeutic process provides an avenue to regenerate the family's creative ability to construct workable alternatives to the problems that they face. From the outset, this process of counseling conveys a sense of hope and optimism for the family; the family is not alone and its members have not been labeled as sick or deviant.

The quoted passage from Hoffman (1988) also points out that this form of counseling is pluralistic. Given the social climate in which families exist during the 1990s, a theoretical approach that accepts difference as the norm generates a feeling of inclusion. Social construction theorists point to the idea that meaning is a socially constructed phenomena (Gergen, 1985). Gergen (1991) challenged the notion that we are autonomous individuals holding independent beliefs and implied instead that our beliefs are highly pliable, changing drastically with changes in our social context. Gergen aptly suggested that the very definition of family is socially constructed and that this definition changes for every family as their social context changes.

Family counselors must therefore recognize that every family's development is influenced by the themes of the society in which they live (Dym & Glenn, 1993). Dym and Glenn, in their book *Couples: Exploring and Understanding the Cycles of Intimate Relationships*, presented the following about the importance of the changing cultural narrative:

> Couples judge themselves by the standards set by the larger culture. These standards are articulated as contemporary parables in films, television, fiction, and popular psychology, as well as in stories told and examples set by parents, teachers, friends, and relatives. Taken all together, these accounts form a Cultural Narrative that presents couples with the conventional wisdom about the right and wrong ways to start out; whether to marry, when, and whom; who in a couple should take the lead in financial matters or in sexual encounter; who should deal with friends and family; how the partners should resolve disputes; and so on. (p. 28)

We would extrapolate these notions about couples to include the entire family. This idea suggests that we each are bombarded with a tremendous amount of information about how we should be. Families themselves create myths about how to be a family, how to love, how to work, what is worthwhile, and so on. All of these "stories" vie for attention in the creation of each new couple and family.

Dym and Glenn (1993) continued with the idea that couples (families) engage the cultural narrative in many ways. In order for counseling to be helpful, we must have a firm understanding about our clients' constructions of themselves, their couplehood, and their family. No longer can we decide that a family is composed of two

White middle-class adults, two darling and appropriately behaving children, a dog, and a fence. If we as counselors arrive at static definitions of family, or of the normal family, the outcomes of counseling for both counselors and clients are likely to be less than optimal.

Is it any wonder that the notion of one Grand Narrative for family life is in question? The whole concept of family has drastically changed over the past two generations. Our clients present us with a never-ending stream of new or different ways of being a family. With the radical changes that have taken place, the idea of an all-encompassing narrative of family life seems ludicrous. Social construction theory gives family counselors permission to both trust and encourage their clients to engage in a process of discovery about the most satisfying way for them to be a family. No longer can we pretend to have the answer for everyone about every issue. However painful the idea of deconstructing the hierarchical relationship that has historically been present in counseling, moving in the direction of lateral relationships with clients may best meet the demands of an ever-changing narrative about life.

Conclusion

Whether or not social construction theory and the resulting clinical applications become mainstays of therapeutic intervention, these ideas will have an impact. Nichols and Schwartz (1995) suggested that this new movement has led to valuable changes in the field. In their overview text of family therapy, they offered a chapter on the contemporary context of family therapy and presented the following perceptions of the lasting changes from the postmodern inquiry:

> (1) the elevation of meaning to a position at least equal in importance to behavioral interaction patterns; (2) increased humility about our theoretical models; (3) increased attention to the values behind our assumptions (including political values); and (4) decreased urgency to change or control people, and increased trust in their own resources. (p. 131)

It is unlikely that social constructionist inquiry represents the end of learning and growth in couple and family counseling. Maybe social constructionism will merely be another in a long line of theoretical formulations about people and families. Whatever the lasting impact of social constructionist inquiry, its propositions are very timely given the massive changes that confront today's families and their counselors.

References

Bateson, G. (1971). *Steps to an ecology of mind.* New York: Ballantine.

Bateson, G., Jackson, D. D., Haley, J., & Weakland, J. (1956). Toward a theory of schizophrenia. *Behavioral Science, 1*, 251–264.

Berger, P., & Luckmann, T. (1966). *The social construction of reality: A treatise in the sociology of knowledge.* New York: Doubleday.

Bertalanffy, L. von. (1968). *General system theory.* New York: George Braziller.

Bowen, M. (1978). *Family therapy in clinical practice.* New York: Jason Aronson.

Braunsberg, A. (Producer), & Ashby, H. (Director). (1979). *Being there* [Film].

Bubenzer, D., West, J., & Boughner, S. (1994). Interview with Michael White and the narrative perspective in therapy. *The Family Journal: Counseling and Therapy for Couples and Families, 2(1)*, 71–83.

Dym, B., & Glenn, M. L. (1993). *Couples: Exploring and understanding the cycles of intimate relationships.* New York: Harper Collins.

Gergen, K. (1985). The social constructionist movement in modern psychology. *American Psychologist, 20*, 266–275.

Gergen, K. (1991). *The saturated self: Dilemmas of identity in contemporary life.* New York: Basic Books.

Haley, J. (1963). *Strategies of psychotherapy.* New York: Grune and Stratton.

Hoffman, L. (1988). A constructivist position for family therapy. *The Irish Journal of Psychology, 9(1)*, 110–129.

Jackson, D. D. (1967). *Therapy, communication, and change.* Palo Alto, CA: Science and Behavior Books.

Kosinski, J. (1971). *Being there.* New York: Bantam.

Lyddon, W. J. (1995). Cognitive therapy and theories of knowing: A social constructionist view. *Journal of Counseling and Development, 73*, 579–595.

McGowan, J. (1991). *Postmodernism and its critics.* Ithaca, NY: Cornell University Press.

Minuchin, S. (1974). *Families and family therapy.* Cambridge, MA: Harvard University Press.

Nichols, M. P., & Schwartz, R. C. (1995). *Family therapy: Concepts and methods.* Boston: Allyn & Bacon.

Norris, C. (1990). *What's wrong with postmoderism: Critical theory and the ends of philosophy.* Baltimore: Johns Hopkins University Press.

Satir, V. (1964). *Conjoint family therapy.* Palo Alto, CA: Science and Behavior Books.

Schweder, R., & Miller, J. (1985). The social construction of the person: How is it possible? In K. Gergen & K. Davis (Eds.), *The social construction of the person* (pp. 41–72). New York: Springer-Verlag.

Shotter, J. (1989). Social accountability and the social construction of "you". In J. Shotter & K. Gergen (Eds.), *Texts of identity* (pp. 133–150). London: Sage.

Skinner, B. F. (1953). *Science and human behavior.* New York: Macmillan.
Skinner, B. F. (1971). *Beyond freedom and dignity.* New York: Knopf.
Tarnas, R. (1991). *The passion of the Western mind.* New York: Ballantine Books.
Watzlawick, P., Beavin, J., & Jackson, D. (1967). *Pragmatics of human communication.* New York: Norton.
Watzlawick, P., & Weakland, J. H. (Eds.). (1977). *The interactional view: Studies at the mental research institute, Palo Alto, 1965–1974.* New York: Norton.
Watzlawick, P., Weakland, J., & Fisch, R. (1974). *Change: Principles of problem formation and problem resolution.* New York: Norton.

PART II

SOCIAL CONSTRUCTION THEORY AND COUNSELING

2

A Solution-Oriented Approach in Couple and Family Counseling

John M. Littrell, EdD
Jeffrey J. Angera, Phd

John: You know, Jeff, we could begin this chapter by presenting a dialogue between the two of us. I think it may give our readers a sense of a solution-oriented (O'Hanlon & Weiner-Davis, 1989) approach to counseling and how it continues to evolve in our postmodern world.

Jeff: I think evolving is a key concept in that solutions aren't permanent, only the next answer. Our dialogue will also serve as a model for how our reflection on the counseling process provides counselors new choices and perspectives. However, I wish there were some way that this dialogue would also include our readers. Readers are so often ignored by authors who seem to have it all worked out. Many authors treat their readers as passive recipients of their insights rather than as active participants who co-create realities.

John: Let's extend an invitation to them to voice their ideas through letters, phone calls, and e-mail so we can begin a dialogue. Here's how to reach us:

Dept. of Professional Studies
N221 Lagomarcino Hall
Iowa State University, Ames, IA 50011

Telephone: (515) 294-5746
Fax: (515) 294-4942
e-mail: jlittrel@iastate

Jeff: I'm feeling more postmodern by the minute in that we are engaged in socially constructing multiple realities and inviting the readers to do the same, rather than trying to uncover a single reality. This mirrors my work with a family I'd like to talk about. But first, we should explain our plan for this chapter. I'm going to tell about a family I worked with for over nine months. To me the case contains many elements that illustrate a solution-oriented approach to counseling. The case will serve as a springboard for illustrating our solution-oriented views of clients, counselors, and the counseling process. I'm wondering, John, if we run the risk of losing some readers in presenting our points in a relatively nonlinear manner.

John: Actually, I think we're talking a language that most counselors are very familiar with, because that is how our clients talk to us about their lives—clients are hardly sequential and orderly in their presentations. You and I can mirror the mosaic-like phenomena that occur in counseling where patterns begin to emerge as the dialogue continues. In addition, we can make explicit the social construction framework as it emerges in the counseling context.

Jeff: Let's also insert, set off with bullets, additional solution-oriented questions which we didn't ask, but which are in keeping with how we operate.

John: To begin, I'd like you to provide some initial background information about the family. We'll alternate between your presentation of the case, narrated in the first person, and our dialogue. This discussion will tease out the various assumptions that underlie the actions you and other professional helpers took in working with this family. In addition to having your case illustrate a solution-oriented approach to counseling, our own dialogue will also serve as a model of a solution-oriented approach. Both of us tend to think in solution-oriented ways, therefore we can model, through our dialogue, how to approach case conceptualization and action in a solution-oriented fashion. Jeff, from what you've already told me about the case, I think we might title it, "The Family From Hell."

Jeff: That title would be an accurate description of how many social service professionals had viewed this family prior to my involvement. They almost had me believing it was true.

However, "The Family From Hell" is a problem-oriented title. I prefer to call the case "Come Together" because that more accurately describes the process the family experienced.

John: Jeff, we can let our readers decide. Why don't you begin by telling us about the family?

I'm a Loser

Jeff: While I was working as an in-home family counselor for a local counseling agency that had contracts with the state, I received an intake folder for a new case. As my supervisor handed me the folder, she smirked and said, "This ought to be a fun one!" Unfortunately, you could cut the sarcasm with a knife. My colleague Rachael (pseudonym), a child development specialist, was assigned to work conjointly on the case. She was to focus on the family's life and social skills, while I was to be the family counselor.

The family was composed of two parents (not married) and five children. All the children (ages 7, 5, 4, 3, and 2) were the biological offspring of Pete (the father) and Wendy (the mother) except the oldest who was Wendy's child from a previous relationship. All five children had been diagnosed and identified as "failure to thrive"—a label given to children who are below the 10th percentile for body weight for their respective ages. The referral paperwork stated that Pete and Wendy lacked parenting skills regarding nutrition, safety, health, nurturing, and discipline. The family's home had a history of being dirty, unsafe, and crowded with other extended family members and friends who would frequently stay in the home when they were experiencing difficulties. Neither parent had completed high school; however, Pete had acquired some skills through his experience as a drywaller. The family's income was very low. Money came from small drywalling jobs Pete secured and from state assistance.

John: We've called this section, "I'm a Loser" because clearly you were presented information that said "this family is a loser." Others seemed to want to convince you that there is a single reality and that this family deserved a label. This single reality view was enforced by a hierarchy with the power to define who and what this family was. I suspect the powers-that-be would say they are simply recognizing reality.

Jeff: I'd go one step further. In my social constructionist view, there were multiple realities, and many of the voices (e.g., father's, mother's, parents', children's) representing those multiple realities were not being heard.

You're Going to Lose That Girl

Jeff: Six months prior to my agency's involvement, all five children were removed from the parents' custody because of allegations of neglect; all five children were placed in foster care. When we first saw them, the children had been court-ordered to be returned home. However, the judge explicitly stated that if the children's health and the well-being of the family did not improve, the children would be permanently removed from the parents' custody—this was their last chance. The judge's ruling for the children to be returned to the home was totally opposite to the recommendations of the professionals involved with the family. After the judge's ruling, the professionals predicted that the family did not have a chance of making it. The case was considered hopeless; my colleague and I were viewed as idealists for even thinking things could change. We were willing to take the risk because of our belief, an assumption of solution-oriented work, that change would occur; it was not a matter of it happening, but a question of how soon.

The family had a long history of involvement in the state's various programs. Concurrent with my agency's involvement, Wendy was enrolled in a parent education program that taught parenting skills, nutrition, and personal hygiene. The children were in a Head Start-like program from 8 to 4 o'clock each day when not in school; the family was visited by a nurse on a biweekly basis to monitor the children's health. Prior to Rachael's and my services, the family had received, over the last two generations, a laundry list of social service programs such as family preservation, assertiveness training, and individual counseling to mention only a few. Because of the complexities of this family's situation and the warnings from other professionals, we entered the case somewhat overwhelmed before ever seeing the family.

Our family's neighborhood was rundown and their rental house matched. As we entered their home, no one rose to greet us. Our presence was minimally acknowledged by head nodding. Pete sat hunched in his chair, his stomach protruding. He had long hair and was unshaved. Dangling from his lips was a cigarette with a one-inch ash. My first impression of this man was that he was the personification of evil. Wendy, a heavy-set woman, sat with no expression staring at the television, which blared throughout the room. The children alternated between wildly running around the room or hanging onto us.

Rachael and I introduced ourselves. We began asking traditional types of questions regarding reasons for our referral such as, "So why do you think we are here?" Pete and Wendy hesitantly replied with one- and two-word answers. We later speculated that we must have seemed to them indistinguishable from all of the other social service professionals who had ceaselessly paraded through their lives over the years.

During our initial home visits we reverted to our former approach in working with families (i.e., convincing them of the legitimacy of our presence and why they should change to meet the state's expectations). For the first month and a half, we worked hard to persuade the family that:

1. junk food had no nutritional value,
2. the parents had to interact with their children to avoid emotional neglect,
3. Pete and Wendy should supervise their children's play activities more,
4. their children had to eat their supper when it was prepared,
5. Pete and Wendy had to talk more as parents about their relationship and how they wanted to parent, and
6. many other "good" suggestions as to how to make their family better should be followed.

Not surprisingly, our implied injunctions to "shape up" fell on unreceptive ears. Things stayed much the same. Our frustration level continued to rise steadily. We had become associated in the parents' eyes with the countless helping professionals who had entered their lives and failed. Fisch, Weakland, and Segal (1982) and Watzlawick, Weakland, and Fisch (1974) have illustrated how clients' attempted solutions which are simply "more-of-the-same" fail to work. As counselors, we are just as susceptible as our clients are to "more-of-the-same" patterns. Clearly, we were now knee-deep in a failed solution.

John: Right from the start of this case, you and Rachael seemed to have headed straight for previously failed solutions. What was happening?

Jeff: Initially, I was influenced by the social worker's language in her case plan. It spelled out in so many words that if the parents screw up this time the court would never let them have custody again. The cards were stacked against them—their odds of succeeding were infinitesimal.

John: This family sounded like it would need lots of luck because they certainly lacked skills.

Jeff: Definitely. Our introduction to this family by way of other professionals' comments and the case records also illustrates how influential language can be in determining a view of reality. Very quickly into this case, I had abandoned my solution-oriented approach. In the face of the parent educator's descriptions of the parents as having "serious trouble" and "lacking motivation," I reverted to my former problem-oriented method of approaching families. This lasted for six weeks.

John: So for six weeks, you believed the "experts" were right. For a while you accepted the modernist's view that "analytical experts" could diagnose and accurately label what reality is (Waters, 1994). How did you escape the experts' negative labels and prognosis for this family?

Jeff: Two things helped—writing a report and consulting colleagues. I had to write a progress report of what we'd done so far. Unfortunately, we weren't seeing much change. I had begun thinking that we had failed and that we were wasting the state's money by continuing to see this family. I remember asking myself, why aren't we seeing change?

John: It was a very discouraging time and also a time for questioning what you were doing.

Jeff: I was confronted by not being able to assist this family and I felt I had let them down. My questioning led me to look to do something different, trying to put me back on a solution-oriented track (Littrell, 1998). I'll continue with more information about the family.

With a Little Help From My Friends

Jeff: In an effort to get unstuck and to do something different, Rachael and I consulted with each other and another colleague, Richard, who also works from a resource-based, solution-oriented framework. Richard's first question was, "What do you two need to do to get back on track?"

- How do you want to be working instead?
- When you are on track with this client, what will you be doing differently?

As we talked, it became obvious that Rachael and I had made several fundamental errors. First, we had allowed the negative referral information and our communications with other professionals involved with the case to persuade us that their way of thinking worked best. We had abandoned our resource-based, solution-oriented approach to working with people. We now realized that we had to change our "lens" and shift from seeing what was not working in the family to what was working. In other words, what were the strengths of this family? What was this family doing that worked? (de Shazer, 1985, 1988). In changing to this orientation, some immediate resources that we had overlooked began to emerge. For example, the parents had stayed together for eight years—there was stability in the relationship. In addi tion, there was no drug use and no drinking, which in their neighborhood bordered on being a miracle.

A second error we had made was accepting the goals we had been given rather than determining what the family's goals were. As we talked, we realized that the goals for this family were precisely that—goals for the family rather than goals with the family. Rachael, Richard, and I began solution-oriented talk such as, "What does this family want?" rather than problem-oriented talk such as, "What are this family's problems?" (Furman & Ahola, 1992).

- When this family is *not* a concern of the state, what will they be doing differently that fits for them?

To correct this second error, we worked with the parents to make the goals meaningful to them. I said to Pete and Wendy, "I bet you're tired of all these professional people marching through your house." Pete answered in a monotone voice,

"Oh, we've gotten used to it." I came back with, "I suspect you two would like to be on your own—have the state get off your backs." Pete and Wendy liked that. I continued, "Does it make sense that we set two goals with the first being get the state off your backs, and the second being focus more on your children?" They agreed that these were goals they wanted.

Framed in this manner, the parents, the state, Rachael, and I were now in agreement about two big goals. The big goals had the effect of making the smaller goals such as increased child supervision seem much more relevant and meaningful. Framed in this way, the small goals that the state had thought the parents should be working on became goals the parents wanted. Their motivation increased.

Our third error was brought to light by Richard when he asked, "How much time have you spent building a relationship with this family?" Rachael and I suddenly realized we had allowed our feelings of being overwhelmed to blind us to a key fact—we had raced to impose a diet consisting of "should," "must," and "have to" on the family. We knew we needed to take time to understand the family's worldviews and to build a relationship based on trust.

To correct our errors, we rethought the treatment plan and changed our own thinking. We decided to incorporate thinking about solutions that built on the strengths of the family. We would implement this new plan not only with the family, but with the other professionals involved with the case. But before all else, Rachael and I went to work on increasing rapport with the family by listening more rather than trying to have them reach our goals.

John: I'd like to respond to several parts of what you've just told me. First, I am fascinated by how you and the parents co-constructed a goal that fit the realities of the parents. It's a rhetorical question, but would I be right in assuming that the state's goal would never have been phrased as getting off the parents' backs?

Jeff: You're right, John. It is a rhetorical question.

John: Second, you spoke of rapport building. I'm reminded about what the bank robber John Dillinger is apocryphally quoted as saying, "You can get so much more out of people with a kind word and a gun, than just a gun." My paraphrase of this for counselors is, "You can get so much more out of people with warmth, genuineness, and empathy and a solution-oriented approach than just a solution-oriented approach." We can't overlook our relationships with our clients because we've become so enamored of our approach and techniques (Duncan, Solovey, & Rusk, 1992).

Jeff: Building rapport with the family was very important. That's something that I still find essential even though I've changed approaches. Occasionally I have caught myself focusing so intently on being solution-oriented that I failed to build the relationship as much as needed. When I do that I find I have to back up and build the foundation of really listening and attending to them.

John: Earlier you mentioned collaborating with other professionals. Just like our theoretical frameworks and favorite techniques can get in the way, so also can the beliefs of other professionals. You faced a need to get support for your solution-oriented plans. I note that collaboration was very useful at this stage.

Jeff: Not just useful, essential. I find I revert to problem-oriented ways of doing counseling unless I have the opportunity to receive support and encouragement from colleagues. This in turn restricts my ability to see resources.

John: When I train counselors in a solution-oriented approach, one of the key elements is providing time to confer with each other and support each other (Littrell et al., 1992; Littrell, Malia, & Vanderwood, 1995). It is so easy to revert to older patterns even when the older patterns may not be as effective.

Jeff: When I get stuck, I seek out colleagues who work from a solution-oriented framework. These people ask me solution-oriented questions that make me think about what I am doing.

- If I were watching a videotape of one of your sessions with this family and you were working from a solution-focused framework, what would I see you doing differently (O'Hanlon & Schultheis, 1992)?
- How will you use your language to channel your clients into solution talk?

When I think in solution-oriented ways about what I am doing, it also helps me to think in solution-oriented ways about what my clients are doing.

John: A variation on the "physician, heal thyself" approach?

Jeff: Yes, it helps me stick with the model rather than being overwhelmed that my clients' problems are too complex or thinking that this approach won't work. My colleagues are encouraging of my acknowledgement of multiple perspectives, especially when traditional approaches (as opposed to postmodern ones) operate with mechanical, linear, causal, deterministic, and objective models (Lincoln & Guba, 1985). I feel I'm in a battle and I'm losing to people who are convinced they have the answer for clients. I get discouraged because my approach is more organismic, mutually causal, indeterminate, and perspective oriented (Lincoln & Guba, 1985).

John: So to be more optimistic, you don't just seek out anyone—you find solution-oriented colleagues as opposed to problem-oriented ones.

Jeff: And when I do, I feel supported, encouraged, and challenged to rethink how I am working. Then I'm more creative and have more energy to get beyond impasses.

Getting Better

Jeff: An initial test of our solution-oriented approach came with the topic of meals. Snacking and meal times were highly problematic, especially considering the concern over the children being malnourished. This was a family who loved junk food. There was no way to make them totally give it up. Rachael and I needed to change our approach; we had to learn to modify our behavior.

We probed for the exceptions to find when the children did eat well (de Shazer, 1988).

- I'm assuming you've had this problem at sometime in the past. What did you do to get them to eat then?
- When is there a time that the children do eat well?

Wendy provided an immediate clue when she said, "If I serve dinner later, the kids eat better. That's because they wear themselves out playing outside." Wendy had been taught in various parenting programs that dinner should be served early in the evening, but with this family that wasn't going to work. We took what worked and attempted to modify it only enough to ensure that the children ate nutritionally.

- So when the kids get all worn out from playing outside they eat a hearty dinner. What do you do to make sure they get all played out?
- How do you get that to happen?

We asked the parents to push their dinner time back by an hour to an hour and a half until the children had sufficient time to wear themselves out playing, then call them to dinner. This way the children didn't miss playing outside. In addition, the children built up a good hunger even though they had snacked earlier. We concentrated on what worked by helping the parents identify special foods that each child liked. We were all working toward the goal of having the children gain weight so they would not be permanently removed from the parents and that the state would get off their backs.

- What are the little tricks you have learned to doctor up their food to get them to eat?

Snacks were also a major problem. However, instead of discouraging snacks, we encouraged them. We made sure that the kids came home immediately after day care and had a snack. These snacks were more limited in amount and healthier—this didn't always work, but many times it did.

John: Sounds like you had to shift gears to find goals that fit more for the family and that they could identify as meaningful, in addition to finding what was working instead of what was not working.

Jeff: Yes! We—Rachael, the parents, and I—all wanted the children to eat, but the parents had been taught by the parent education program that dinner had to be at 5:30 p.m. It just didn't work having the kids come home from day care and school, eat a big snack of potato chips and candy, and then expect them to eat a nutritious dinner in another two hours.

John: You're saying the solution generated (and it appears imposed) by the parent education program didn't work for this family.

Jeff: You bet. The whole family, parents on down, all protected that afternoon snack. It was a ritual. We had to realize that the 5:30 p.m. mealtime solution, though it might fit our worldviews, wasn't going to fit for the family.

John: You acknowledged multiple realities rather than a single reality that could be imposed. How did you help the family do something different?

Jeff: It was actually quite simple—I listened. I asked the parents, "What would be some possible times you could get the kids to eat a healthy dinner?" My question assumed the goal could be achieved. They both paused for a moment and then Wendy fortuitously said, "When they are worn out from playing." I asked when that happened and Wendy replied, "When they stay out playing later. It's summer and the sun is out longer." I thought to myself, "That's it!"

John: So they had their own solution; you just needed to make it more salient.

Jeff: That's right. They had their own solution, but because it was drilled into them at parent education program that the kids had to eat at 5:30 p.m., they didn't pay attention to their experience. All we did from that point on was continue to remind them that the big goal was to keep their kids and get the State off their backs—part of that involved the weight gain of the children. If they were eating healthier dinners we would be assured they would be moving in the direction of the goal. I complimented them on their new solution and kept encouraging them to pay attention to what works. With additional support and modeling from Rachael during the dinner hour, the family started to develop a new pattern.

John: A major focus was making overt the patterns that the family had socially constructed as effective, not those you as a counselor thought should be effective. You explored patterns that work or have worked, rather than those that didn't work. That's a real change of focus. You looked for exceptions that worked in the past (de Shazer, 1985, 1988).

Jeff: And in looking for past exceptions that worked, we found them. I have continually found that families and couples have engaged in useful patterns in the past, but that these are not being used in the present. Sometimes they have just forgotten patterns that have previously worked.

- When the state sees the kids gaining weight they will be convinced you are focusing more on your children and then they will get off your back. What will you be doing when this happens?

I find that when clients rediscover previous patterns that have worked that they are excited and that their sense of hope increases. I have turned to de Shazer (1988) and Walter and Peller (1992) for excellent examples of encouraging exceptions.

All You Need Is Love

Jeff: Pete and Wendy were having some difficulty in their relationship. In discussing how they handled their differences, Pete stated that he would leave the house when things got heated. My first reaction was to assume he was a conflict avoider and to try to work on conflict management skills. As it turned out, Pete and Wendy had jointly developed a very specific solution that worked for them and was based on a sound rationale.

Pete would leave home to cool down because he knew he had a hot temper. He didn't want to explode in front of the children or become abusive with Wendy. After cooling down, he and Wendy would get back together and talk about their differences in a way that was sufficient for them—maybe not for me as the counselor, but more significantly, it worked for them as a couple. Important for them was the fact that they did not get into heated arguments in front of their children. We framed this as yet another sign that the parents were concerned about their children.

- How does your leaving the house during an argument show that you are concerned about what your children are exposed to?

When it came time to protect the children from the parents' disagreements, the parents had a solution that worked. It was hard for me to see it as a solution since I framed leaving the house as avoidance or abandonment. My own middle-class background said that husbands don't walk out. This family taught me once again that there are many solutions and that mine don't work for all families. I keep gaining more respect for the solutions that families and couples come up with. I listen intently to their strengths.

John: I can see where Pete's walking out challenged your own values. This couple's solution flies in the face of many theories of how to manage conflicts in a relationship.

Jeff: Doesn't it though? Let me tell you, when we first started talking about the relationship problems and I heard avoidance as their solution, my first reaction was to give them all my counselor knowledge about the "therapeutically approved" ways to handle relationship difficulties. Fortunately, I caught myself and I chose to become a curious counselor, rather than the one with the answers.

John: A postmodern point of view would hold that we construct our futures with better materials when we use strengths and resources rather than deficits. How did you stop yourself from delivering a "packaged" solution and start being curious about their solutions?

Jeff: At times it's hard to stop. One thing that cues me to switch gears is when I find myself working harder than my client. In solution-oriented counseling, clients tend to work hard because they see results rather quickly. If I'm viewing myself as working harder than my clients, I realize that I'm trying to sell them my answers and not listening to theirs.

When I switched gears from being critical to being curious with this family, it led to more supportive evidence for why these parents should retain custody of their children. They didn't grow up in an environment that expressed feelings publicly, so to expect them to have a "June and Ward Cleaver" discussion was out of the question. Their solution worked in their context.

John: So for them, cooling off and not exploding in front of the kids was important and communicated their consideration for their children. I see this as a wonderful example of using the clients' worldview as a starting point for dialogue. Seems like you extended the dialogue by reframing avoidance behavior as concerned behavior (Cade & O'Hanlon, 1993).

Jeff: Exactly. And they agreed with the new construction.

John: There's a good lesson in that—if it works, don't fix it (deShazer, 1985). Plus, you successfully met the challenge of putting aside your inherent bias and accepting their way of living that worked for them, even though it would never fit for you. Isn't it interesting how we in the helping professions sometimes assume we're the experts on our clients' lives?

Jeff: That's the challenge when working from a solution-oriented perspective because we can't assume that we have the answer or even answers. It's a co-creating process. We take our solution process expertise and blend it with the family's expertise on their lives, and it's amazing how people start to realize they have all the resources they need to work toward their goals. In some instances it just requires us to get out of their way.

John: I use the phrase, "Clients are so much more knowledgeable about their worlds than I'll ever be." I'm continually learning more about how to trust my clients to know what will fit. I think that's the most powerful lesson that Carl Rogers and Milton Erickson independently taught—trust your clients to have many internal strengths and help them use them.

We Can Work It Out

Jeff: When the children got into trouble, we suggested, from our framework, that the family use "time outs" by putting the child in the corner for the number of minutes equal to his or her age. The parents said this didn't work. So we asked them, "What would work?" They said, "We put them in their rooms and make them lie down on their beds until we say they can come out."

- What have you used in the past that has been effective?

At first, this didn't seem like much of a difference to us; however, to the parents and children it was a meaningful difference. Since the parents, Rachael, and I had something that worked, we could build on it and discover ways to make it more effective. This led to solutions regarding how the parents could show support for each other when the children were disciplined in this manner.

- What were the good things that happened when you made them lie down on their beds?

- How do you keep them from acting out more when you send them to their beds? And then what do you do?
- What changes in their behavior do you see that tells you this is a good method of disciplining?

John: I'm constantly amazed at how "an unrecognized difference becomes a difference that make a difference" (de Shazer, 1988, p. 10). Families seem to have a rather intuitive knowledge about what will work for them if we will only listen.

Jeff: Often I find my role is to help people believe in themselves. By emphasizing what I hear them saying they begin the process of trusting themselves. I amplify their tentative ideas about what works (O'Hanlon & Weiner-Davis, 1989).

- What do you notice about yourselves and your children when you are more confident in the way you discipline your children?
- What do other people notice?

John: You almost sound like a cheerleader (Gingerich, de Shazer, & Weiner-Davis, 1988).

Jeff: Cheerleader?

John: Repeatedly you've told me about how you encourage clients to try new things or continue some behaviors they are already doing. Even as we talk you are enthusiastic. You're also highly supportive of their making changes.

Jeff: Guess you're right. I do pull for the people I work with. In this family, an example of cheerleading would be when I supported Wendy's ideas of how to get the children to eat her nutritious meals. Anything other than potato chips and candy would have been a move in the right direction for these children.

- When have you observed your children eating your nutritious meals?
- What have you done in the past that has worked most effectively?

After some questions about times when the children would eat, Wendy noted a significant exception. Her youngest child ate better when gravy was spread over the food on his plate. When she told me how this exception worked, I said, "That's great! You must really know your children to find solutions that work like that." Wendy then added, "My youngest really likes his food soupy—things like granola with yogurt spread on top." Again, I congratulated her on finding solutions that worked for her children.

John, as an aside, Rachael and I both recognized that gravy is not the world's most perfect food; however, Wendy's use of it to get her youngest to eat turkey was considered by us a significant movement in the direction of better nutrition for the children—much better than candy and chips. In other words, I don't look for perfect answers to bad situations, but better solutions to undesired problems. I focus on small steps in the process rather than end results.

John: I really appreciate your enthusiasm with this family. You're not a detached clinician. In our talks about this family, I've heard you use phrases such as, "No kidding!" "That's great!" "How did you do that?" and "I don't get it because I was here just last week . . . and now there are these new things happening."

Jeff: But it's so much more than words. I really do get enthusiastic. I really do pull for the people I work with. My social construction perspective holds that clients are not the problem, rather the problem is separate from the client and that I can work with the client to deal with the problem (White & Epston, 1990). A lot of my cheerleading is nonverbal and paraverbal. If I couldn't move my arms and hands when I talk, I couldn't function. When I'm solution-oriented and enthusiastic, my clients begin to, as they say in baseball, catch the fever.

Little Child

Jeff: One of the state's main concerns involved parental neglect. An example of this was the perceived lack of parental supervision of the children's activities—these were little children. From my middle-class point of view, I tended to concur on this matter. Once again, this illustrated how my middle-class lens blurred my vision as I overlooked some valuable resources that the family was using to meet this need. When I questioned Wendy regarding the children's supervision, she matter-of-factly commented that she and the neighbor woman who lived two doors down often worked together to watch the children.

- Who, besides Pete, helps you watch the kids?

This neighbor had two children who were close in age to Wendy 's children. The two families provided a supportive network for each other. Wendy and the neighbor would alternate supervision of outdoor play activities or jointly care for the children. Once again, my cultural value system constricted my conceptualization of the situation. I held the belief that each nuclear family provided all care for its own children. Quite the contrary, in the lower socioeconomic neighborhood that Wendy and Pete's family lived in, the close network of adults cooperated to care for children.

John: This is another instance when the clients already had a solution in place and you had to step back and question the assumptions that you brought into the counseling situation.

Jeff: Yes. My nuclear family orientation got in the way of seeing the strength of alternative solutions. That's why I think it's so important to have an awareness and be knowledgeable about social and cultural differences that exist in our society. Otherwise, I could easily fall into the trap of imposing my solutions on others.

John: My experience in teaching about solution-oriented counseling has convinced me that the hardest part for counselors is not learning the techniques. Counselors learn the techniques rather quickly. What is considerably more difficult is acquiring a framework where we set aside our theoretical frameworks and our culturally encapsulated perspectives so as to see what is working in clients' lives. Our theories have been so problem focused that we tend to believe that unless we thoroughly understand the problem we can't assist someone. A solution-oriented approach moves as quickly as possible to finding out what people want, what is working, and has worked. A solution-oriented approach assists clients in constructing new realities using many different methods.

Jeff: The more Rachael and I worked with Pete, Wendy, and their children, the more they amazed us with their solutions. Rachael and I simply had to amplify their solutions. The "cooperating neighbors" is another instance when our client already had a solution in place and we had to step back and look at the assumptions we were bringing to counseling. It's amazing how difficult it is to transcend the worldviews we subscribe to. The challenge from a solution-oriented perspective is recognizing how our perceptions of how life "should be" may differ dramatically from our clients' perceptions.

John: And through this awareness process, we can free ourselves by recognizing we don't have to fit clients to our template. So often we are trained to label clients as "resistant" and "in denial" if they don't conform to our belief system (Berg & Miller, 1992).

Jeff: In this instance, my personal beliefs may have led me to correct the family's parenting practices by attempting to instruct them on proper supervision. However, I consciously stepped back and asked, "What works for you?"

John: It's almost like that question allowed you to remove your self-imposed ear plugs and really listen to strategies the family already had in place.

Jeff: My job suddenly became much easier. Instead of attempting to dramatically alter parenting practices, I simply had to compliment them and make them aware of what they were doing.

John: And how did you go about doing that?

Jeff: Again, I reminded them of the larger goals we had mutually agreed on: keeping custody of the children and getting the state off their backs. I went on to link these overarching goals to this strategy of supervision. I said, "So this is an example of how you are providing good care for your children. This shows you are putting the children at the center. That tells the state you are good parents and should maintain custody. So how are we going to make sure this way of supervising the kids works even better?"

John: So you systematically linked the specific activity to the larger goal and used "—ing" words to denote process rather than end results. I also noticed you used the word "we" in the last statement. This seems to illustrate how you consider yourself part of the process of co-creating a situation that will ensure the family reaches their larger goal. This is another example of how powerful language can be.

Help!

Jeff: It was obvious that Wendy faced formidable obstacles in getting all of the children to sit at the table and eat. Considering the failure to thrive condition that the children had experienced in the past, getting them to eat nourishing food was of utmost concern to the parents and us. Despite the desired goals, the children balked; they would whine about what they had to eat, squirm about, and in no time be running around the table playing with their food.

Our first step to address this problem involved Rachael scheduling her visits concurrent with their dinner time. Since Rachael was working with the family's skill development, she found that being there worked better than teaching at a distance. Rachael would sit patiently, modeling different methods of "parenting persuasion" for Wendy. It was obvious that Wendy couldn't handle the dinner hour alone; however, Rachael told me she wasn't about to move in with them!

During the evening meal, Pete would remain removed from the table in his normal position in front of the television. I hypothesized that success would involve encouraging Pete to become an active participant in the dinner ritual. I'll admit that in my frustrated state I wanted to say to Pete, "If you would get off your ass and stop watching television and sit at the table, then maybe your kids will eat better." Knowing that it wouldn't work, I restrained my anger. I asked myself, how can I support this man? What is he doing that works?

As is often the case when working from a solution-oriented framework, I attempted to elicit Pete's cooperation through compliments. I said, "You know, I'm amazed at how those kids listen to you! I'm not sure what it is, but they really move when you get involved. And you know, I've noticed that they listen to Wendy more when you are around! I bet dinner goes a hell of a lot easier for Wendy, and those kids eat more, when you come in and lay down the law." Within a few days, Wendy's hopeless attitude regarding mealtime began to change; she felt some support from Pete. It took some time and constant encouragement to promote the development of this pattern, but the parents did begin to comment on how mealtimes had become somewhat easier.

Cooperation is so important in working with families. I use every opportunity to make sure that my clients and I are working with each other as cooperatively as possible. Cooperation is a wonderful tool for facilitating the construction of new realities.

John: One way you did that was by complimenting Pete. You seized on a small but meaningful action of his and you amplified it. You noticed it and brought it to his attention.

- Do you think about it or does it just naturally happen?
- What is the first thing you're aware of when you do that thing that works with your kids?
- How much do you congratulate yourself when you succeed in helping your kids in that way?

Jeff: One way I do this is to think small. I look for meaningful patterns that highlight cooperation and caring. I let my clients know that these are really important acts. If I'm going to err when giving compliments, it's because I'm going to give too many rather than too few.

John: Your compliments really work for your clients because they are specific, genuine, and an example of your caring.

Jeff: Thanks, John. That compliment felt good.

Carry That Weight

Jeff: After taking time to understand the family and understand how they saw the world, we moved into a discussion of family history. As it turned out, Wendy and some of her siblings had been removed from her mother's custody when they were children. From a problem-oriented approach, my response would have been, "This is an intergenerational pattern and will not likely change." Immediately, however, I found the positive in the most negative and commented, "Wow! You must know what these kids went through. I bet you are really motivated to make sure that they are not taken away from you for good!" Wendy responded emphatically, "Oh, you bet. I know what it's like and they are not going to take my kids again! I know next time it will be for good."

This exchange opened the door to further discussion of strategies that the family could continue and could improve on to ensure the maintenance of custody. In addition, I think it helped the parents articulate why their children were so important to them.

John: So you took time to consider intergenerational patterns that had impacted the family.

Jeff: Yes, in fact, this short scenario doesn't shed light on the solution-oriented genogram process that I was using (Kuehl, 1995).

John: And by that you mean?

Jeff: As you know, more traditional models of working with families often involve examining familial factors that are transmitted from one generation to the next. Individuals often place a significant amount of importance on, "My parents were this way, so I am too." Unfortunately, too often family-of-origin approaches can highlight family's deficits across generations rather than their strengths.

John: Instead, you used this same framework, but asked solution-oriented questions to focus on strengths that have been passed down across generations? The highlighting of strengths from the past is a fascinating way of providing new perspectives for coauthoring the future with clients (White & Epston, 1990).

- What are you doing that your mom didn't do?
- Your mom was not given a second chance to regain custody of her children like you have been. How have you convinced the state that you deserve this chance?
- What have you learned from your childhood that is valuable to you in the present situation?

Jeff: Yes, and also to point to significant positive changes that have happened from one generation to the next. The future is being constructed even as the past is rewritten.

John: So in this example you focused on how Wendy's experience of being removed from her own mother's custody had become a motivation for her to break the pattern. Instead of becoming a foreteller of doom, you illuminated her motivation for change.

Jeff: Yes, it's almost like the famous print "Day and Night" by M. C. Escher who used the principle of figure/ground. One person can study the print and the predominant images they see are white birds flying to the right. Another person can look at the same print and see black birds flying to the left. The two images are woven together in such a manner that one can choose to attend to either image—it's a matter of training the eye to see from multiple points of view.

John: In much the same way, a counselor may view intergenerational patterns and only see the passing down of deficits, or the counselor may be aware of the family's strengths by asking questions that focus on strengths and resources.

- How have you managed to make things better?
- How are you already dealing with this problem better than your parents did? (Kuehl, 1995)
- What can you learn from that bad episode in your life that can help you in the present?

Questions of this type begin to help the family rewrite their past from one of failures to one of successes. They start to believe they can make it.

All Together Now

Jeff: When working with families I typically ask about family rituals. It seems that families are often unaware of common behaviors, events, or activities that they share. This is particularly the case around the holidays.

When I first posed the question about rituals, Pete and Wendy were not exactly sure what I meant. I rephrased and asked "What are some fun things you do around the holidays?" Apparently *holiday* was the key word. They became more animated than they ever had before! Wendy went on to tell about their plans for going trick-or-treating with the children, the costumes she had found, the neighborhood they would "hit" for candy, and the friends who would share in the fun. Pete then picked up and talked about how they planned to decorate the evergreen tree in the front yard, all the blinking Christmas lights they purchased, and the different kinds of fudge they made each year.

It was obvious that the family had many rituals, however, they simply didn't conceptualize them in that way. With one simple question, we were able to move into a discussion about how participating in family rituals and holidays was yet another sign of family togetherness and good parenting.

John: This discussion sounds as if it were a major turning point.

Jeff: Imber-Black and Roberts (1992) have written about the use of ritual in families as a means of creating community. I relabeled ritual as "holiday" for the family and that had significant meaning for them. Our discussion moved to rich descriptions of meaningful shared family time that was focused on the children's enjoyment.

John: I'm guessing this presented fertile ground for illustrating resources the family possessed, particularly with this family. Many counselors would hold a goal for this family of creating more cohesion among its members. This family didn't talk that kind of language. They talked Christmas trees and presents and in the process they moved closer together.

Jeff: Many meaningful discussions presented themselves as we planned for the holidays. For instance, we developed a plan for the parents to save money and tap area resources to ensure they could participate in the activities planned.

- So how are you tucking away money to make sure you can do these fun things as a family?

And again, working from our solution-oriented framework, we highlighted these activities as indicators that we were moving in the direction of their longer-range goals of child custody and maintenance and getting the state off their backs.

John: That's an important point—continually linking specific behaviors to the larger goal. I use the phrase, "So doing (a specific behavior) lets us know you are moving in the right direction toward your (client's goal)." Also, it appears that you took the opportunity to make this more than just a pleasant discussion by connecting these family activities to other aspects of living beyond the holiday. After all, everyone needs something to strive for.

Jeff: There was real joy in that moment of making fudge and at the same time knowing it was an indication that the family was pulling together. Incidentally, John, the fudge was almost unpalatable, but I relished the family's change.

John: Next!

Hello, Goodbye

Jeff: The children had developed quite a liking for Rachael. The children and the parents knew that she was working to ensure they would achieve their goal of maintaining custody. When she would arrive at the home the children would cling to her pleading that she pick them up, pulling and tugging until they got her undivided attention (which was difficult considering there were five children). At first Rachael tolerated the inappropriate greetings, thinking this behavior would soon diminish. However, after some time there was little change in the clinging behavior. Rachael began responding to the behavior by saying, "I'm happy to see you also, and I don't think we need to crawl all over each other. How do we show each other that we are happy to see each other without crawling on each other?" This question led to identifying a few specific behaviors—some of which they already were doing—which included the children opening Rachael's car door when she would arrive, escorting her into the house holding her hand, and then showing her their projects from day care or their special toys. The same escorting process was repeated when she left the house.

This example illustrates that the search for solutions isn't limited to adults. The children were active participants in identifying and generating other ways to show and receive attention.

John: It seems that this was a little more directive approach than one might use with adults, and yet Rachael still looked for solutions that would fit for the children.

Jeff: Rachael often talks about setting boundaries with children and then trying to generate options that they can choose from (Gil, 1991).

John: In effect, the generation of solutions is more contingent on the adults, yet children still have the ability to make choices that fit best with them.

Jeff: Rachael indicated that this approach gave the children a sense of involvement. In addition to her directly saying, "Don't do that," Rachael would teach the children how to do new behaviors or increase existing behaviors, such as how to respect other people's space and positive ways to show affection.

John: And once you give kids a chance they really surprise you with their imagination. One aspect of solution-oriented counseling I find commendable is its emphasis on choices—both having people generate more choices and then having them choose which ones will work for them. I note also that Rachael appeared to have used with the children a behavioral approach within your overall solution-oriented approach.

Jeff: Correct. The solution-oriented approach with its multiple-perspective framework doesn't rule out operating at times in a linear, causal, and mechanistic framework if that is appropriate. One can be eclectic in the best sense of the word when it comes to choosing methods to help clients reach their goals.

Tell Me What You See

Jeff: One of the case objectives involved "making the children the center." In essence, the state wanted to see that the parents were giving their children enough attention so as to ensure that their basic needs were being met. During the early phases, the children would climb on the parents and pester them for attention but would receive little acknowledgement or affection in return. Only after we made our paradigmatic shift from problem oriented to solution oriented did we see changes in the interactions among the parents and children.

A telling incident occurred late in the fall of the year. I entered the house to find the family sitting around the television with all eyes glued to the tube. At first glance, nothing appeared different. Suddenly I was aware that I was seeing a metaphor for change that had occurred in the family. Right beside the television which occupied a center spot in the room was a coffee table. On the table I saw the family's new "shrine"—five 8 x 10 inch glossy photographs of all the children. Looking over at the family, I saw Pete seated on my left with the youngest boy nestled in his lap. On my right was Wendy playing pat-a-cake with one of their daughters. I commented on the photographs and Wendy proceeded to tell me the stories behind each picture. The family had done it—they had made the children the center!

John: You talked about a shift from problem to solution orientation. Elaborate on that.

Jeff: We are quite adept at identifying exactly what isn't working or what other people's problems are. If you consider that meaning is constructed through interaction with others, we must realize that as counselors we cannot avoid intervening with our clients. I am invested in the assumption that the counselor's focus on problems and deficits will influence the family to make these same shortcomings forefront in their minds.

John: Yes, and before you know it, clients will start to believe our expertise regarding their problems. Likewise, we can choose to use our influence to co-create a reality with the family that highlights the resources they possess and their competence in finding solutions that will work for them (Durrant & Kowalski, 1993; Waters & Lawrence, 1993).

Jeff: That's exactly what happened in this family. It wasn't as though we came and waved a magic wand and did some fancy techniques to change them. Rather, this family reauthored their story (White & Epston, 1990) regarding the care of their children. We (Rachael, the parents, and myself) worked to co-create a reality that they were good parents and they did put their children first.

John: And once this reality was created they began to behave in a manner that was consistent with this new reality.

Jeff: You bet! I walked into their living room and those photographs were a delightful metaphor that illustrated they believed that the children were the center of the family.

John: It seems that the focus on solutions, resources, and small change at the behavioral level leads to greater change in how people view themselves (Walter & Peller, 1992).

Jeff: I'm reminded that the photographs were also a tool we used in creatively measuring the changes occurring for the family. Although we had objective measures such as the children's weight to know if certain changes were occurring, we also used the photographs to qualitatively assess positive movement. The photos demonstrated as well as anything that this family was getting its act together—all we had to do was look at the prominently displayed photographs to see that Pete and Wendy were increasingly becoming family oriented.

The Long and Winding Road

Jeff: As I reflect back over this case, one important factor that I haven't mentioned yet is how hard we worked to influence other professionals' attitudes and behaviors toward the family. Working with a solution-oriented approach isn't just for families; it's a viable way of working for change in the many systems that influence a couple or family. I'm a part of that system and so are my colleagues. We can also apply a solution-oriented approach to our own involvement.

In my struggles to help this family, I used the Mental Research Institute's (Fisch, Weakland, & Segal, 1982) question, "Who is my client?" The answers were the family (both immediate and extended) and the Department of Social Services (represented by a social worker, a health nurse, the state's guardian/lawyer for the children).

I contacted these various representatives in person, by phone, and in writing. A key aspect of these contacts was my use of solution-oriented language, both oral and written. For example, in my written treatment plans, I took the following sentence (that I would have written before becoming solution oriented),

> OLD: "The family is resistant to eliminating children's snacking behavior despite repeated attempts by us to discourage this and to encourage regular mealtimes"

and transformed it into this:

> NEW: "The children's snacking behavior has been decreased and the move to a later mealtime has ensured that the children are now receiving well-balanced meals that guarantee their needed weight gain."

John: What do you see as the differences between the old and new statements?

Jeff: I think it illustrates several aspects of solution-oriented language. First, in the new quote I avoided pejorative labeling such as "resistant" or other deficit concepts. I see the concept of "resistance" as accenting their failure, rather than providing me clues as to what I could do differently to elicit their cooperation (Selekman, 1993).

John: Good point. Here, have an M&M. Oops! The old behaviorist in me is coming out.

Jeff: The second statement also ties changes that are occurring to specific goals. It says how the family is moving in the direction of their goal, rather than how they have not yet reached it.

John: Over the years, de Shazer (1985, 1988, 1991, 1994) has repeatedly emphasized the power of words in shaping realities. I share his assumptions that we as counselors are active partners with our clients in co-creating new realities. Language is one major tool to accomplish that end. It sounds like this case is coming to a conclusion. What happened next?

Come Together

Jeff: Over the last few months Rachael and I had considerably less involvement with the family as they began to demonstrate they could care for their children in ways that met the state's standards. No bad news was good news and the gains, both in the children's weight and in the care the parents now showed for their children, were substantive. After nine months, involvement with this family, Rachael and I, pleased with their progress, recommended to the social worker that this family no longer needed our services; she concurred with our recommendation. Then the social worker added, "I'm amazed at how fast this case has been closed. A case like this typically takes two years."

John: You covered a lot of ground with this family. I can understand why you changed the title of the case from "The Family From Hell" to "Come Together." They really did! What did you like best about how you and Rachael worked?

Jeff: For one, I was pleased that despite initially detouring into a problem-oriented approach, we caught ourselves and then stayed on a solution-oriented track.

John: Nice use of recovery skills. What else?

Jeff: We focused on what worked for the family—their strengths and resources. For example, when we discovered that the family's supervision of their children playing in the yard was better than we expected, we supported the solutions they had generated.

John: It's easy to notice what doesn't work because the problem is right there. It's more difficult to notice strengths and resources because they are not salient like the problem is.

Jeff: Another thing I liked was how we worked to get a goal that really fit for the family and for the state. We had the family and the state, and we walked the line to satisfy both. We found a way to take the state's imposed goals and transform them into goals that the parents found meaningful.

John: I noticed more change occurred when you framed the goals as meaningful to them. I was also aware that you incorporated some techniques from other theoretical frameworks. How does this reconcile with a solution-oriented approach?

Jeff: I hold an assumption that a solution-oriented approach is a most valuable framework for assisting clients, but there are unlimited techniques and methods that can be used within a solution-oriented approach to help people reach their goals. Genograms and skill teaching can be used in a solution-oriented manner.

I find it highly respectful of people to emphasize their resources and strengths. It holds out the hope of change in ways that problem-oriented approaches promise but do not go after in a direct fashion. However, before I get too carried away, I suggest we draw our dialogue to a close.

John: O.K. I believe that solution-oriented counseling embodies the spirit of a social construction framework and that you've illustrated with numerous concrete examples how the broad framework is translated into action. We've discussed the following 12 ideas from the social construction framework in the context of your case:

1. There are multiple realities, and many voices must be heard from.
2. The future is a co-created process.
3. Language shapes our realities so we need to use language carefully.
4. There are multiple hierarchies, and the expertise of all parties must be recognized.
5. People's goals are mutually determined, not hierarchically imposed by "those who know best."
6. Rapport facilitates sharing realities and building consensus.
7. Focusing on strengths and resources is a more effective way of creating the future than focusing on deficits.
8. A "packaged solution" is an oxymoron.
9. Reframing is a tool for creating alternative realities.
10. The person is not the problem, rather, the problem is the problem.
11. Cooperation is an invaluable tool for defining problems, selecting goals, and implementing methods.
12. Temporary solutions are required because life is always changing.

John: I could continue to be solution oriented, Jeff, but our "in-print" time is up. Let's end knowing that we're continuing to point toward solution-oriented options. Thanks, Jeff.

Jeff: It's been useful to me to talk in a solution-oriented manner about the family I worked with. Even as we've talked I've created new options for how I'll work with families in the future. Thanks, John.

Both John and I would like to continue co-creating the future by engaging you, the reader, in an ongoing dialogue. We invite you to continue this dialogue by contacting us with your ideas.

References

Berg, I. K., & Miller, S. D. (1992). *Working with the problem drinker: A solution-focused approach.* New York: Norton.

Cade, B., & O'Hanlon, W. H. (1993). *A brief guide to brief therapy.* New York: Norton.

de Shazer, S. (1985). *Keys to solution in brief therapy.* New York: Norton.

de Shazer, S. (1988). *Clues: Investigating solutions in brief therapy.* New York: Norton.

de Shazer, S. (1991). *Putting difference to work.* New York: Norton.

de Shazer, S. (1994). *Words were originally magic.* New York: Norton.

Duncan, B. L., Solovey, A. D., & Rusk, G. S. (1992). *Changing the rules: A client-directed approach to therapy.* New York: Guilford Press.

Durrant, M., & Kowalski, K. (1993). Enhancing views of competence. In S. Friedman (Ed.), *The new language of change: Constructive collaboration in psychotherapy* (pp. 107–137). New York: Guilford Press.

Fisch, R., Weakland, J. H., & Segal, L. (1982). *The tactics of change: Doing therapy briefly.* San Francisco: Jossey-Bass.

Furman, B., & Ahola, T. (1992). *Solution talk: Hosting therapeutic conversations.* New York: Norton.

Gil, E. (Speaker). (1991). *Family dynamics and child abuse* [Cassette Recording]. Walnut Creek, CA: Launch Press.

Gingerich, W.J., de Shazer, S., & Weiner-Davis, M. (1988). Constructing change: A research view of interviewing. In E. Lipchik (Ed.), *Interviewing* (pp. 21–32). Rockville, MD: Aspen

Imber-Black, E., & Roberts, J. (1992). *Rituals for our times: Celebrating, healing, and changing our lives and our relationships.* New York: Harper Collins.

Kuehl, B. P. (1995). The solution-oriented genogram: A collaborative approach. *Journal of Marital and Family Therapy, 21,* 239–250.

Lincoln, Y. S., & Guba, E. G. (1985). *Naturalistic inquiry.* Newbury Park, CA: Sage.

Littrell, J. M. (1998). *Brief counseling in action.* New York: Norton.

Littrell, J. M., Malia, J. A., Nichols, R., Olson, J., Nesselhuf, D., & Crandell, P. (1992). Brief counseling: Helping counselors adopt an innovative counseling approach. *The School Counselor, 39,* 171–175.

Littrell, J. M., Malia, J. A., & Vanderwood, M. (1995). Single-session brief counseling in a high school. *Journal of Counseling and Development, 73,* 451–458.

O'Hanlon, W. H., & Schultheis, G. M. (1992). *Brief therapy coach.* Santa Fe, NM: ThirdHand Software.

O'Hanlon, W. H., & Weiner-Davis, M. (1989). *In search of solutions: A new direction for psychotherapy.* New York: Norton.

Selekman, M. D. (1993). *Pathways to change: Brief therapy solutions with difficult adolescents.* New York: Guilford Press.

Walter, J., & Peller, J. (1992). *Becoming solution-focused in brief therapy.* New York: Brunner/Mazel.
Waters, D. (1994). Prisoners of our metaphors: Do dialogic therapies make other methods obsolete? *The Family Therapy Networker, 18,*(6), 73–75.
Waters, D. B., & Lawrence, E. C. (1993). *Competence, courage, and change: An approach to family therapy.* New York: Norton.
Watzlawick, P., Weakland, J. H., & Fisch, R. (1974). *Change: Principles of problem formulation and problem resolution.* New York: Norton.
White, M., & Epston, D. (1990). *Narrative means to therapeutic ends.* New York: Norton.

Acknowledgements

We thank Laura Angera and Jeff Kerber for their solution-oriented assistance with this family.

■ ■ ■

3

A Narrative Perspective on Counseling With Couples and Families

John D. West, EdD
Donald L. Bubenzer, PhD
Jacqueline A. Walsh, MS
Hande Sensoy, MEd

It has been noted that some social scientists align themselves with what is referred to as the "text analogy," and they suggest that "in order to make sense of our lives and to express ourselves, experience must be 'storied' and it is this storying that determines the meaning ascribed to experience" (White & Epston, 1990, pp. 9–10). It is through stories that we locate ourselves individually and collectively in history. We know that stories exist because they affect us, raising thoughts and feelings and related actions. We have been moved by those stories that people have generated from their life experiences. For example, in an effort to highlight the significance of the texts or stories in our lives, two of us have found meaning in what for lack of a better phrase might be termed the "rural life," and perhaps not surprisingly, we have enjoyed segments of Kathleen Norris's (1993) narrative on her life in the western Dakotas:[1]

---

[1]Excerpted from *DAKOTA*. Copyright © 1993 by Kathleen Norris. Reprinted by permission of Ticknor & Fields/Houghton Mifflin Co. All rights reserved.

In fact, the ruggedly independent Dakotas have always been more or less a colony in America, remarkably dependent on outside interests. I feel it everytime I sell wheat for less than it costs to produce, or when I sell the grass-fed cattle of my grandparents' herd to be fattened and pumped full of chemicals in a feed-lot. Our cherished idol, local control, makes us more, not less, vulnerable to manipulation by outside interests. When the farm crisis deepened in the mid-1980s and First Bank Systems pulled out of Lemmon, the article in our weekly newspaper spoke about how wonderful it was that local people were going to have the chance to invest in and run their own bank. In the Minneapolis *Tribune* the bank's move out of small towns such as ours was described as enabling it to provide more "sophisticated consumer services" to urban and suburban Minnesotans. The *Wall Street Journal* applauded First Bank's decision as part of a strategy to drop agricultural loans. The Dakotas make a curious colony for America, but the mystique has been there at least since 1876, when Custer rode out of Mandan to his doom, and Wild Bill Hickok was shot in a saloon in Deadwood. Later on, the young Teddy Roosevelt tried out the life of a cowboy in the North Dakota Badlands. Fueled by dime novels and western movies, most recently *Dances With Wolves* and *Thunderheart*, the appeal of Dakota has never died out, and is apparently inexhaustible in Europe, judging from the number of starstruck Europeans who venture across Highway 12 every summer, passing through Lemmon on their way to Montana or the Black Hills.

For those of us who have a healthy respect for summer heat waves and the violent storms they generate, the Dakota mystique can wear thin in a hurry. One year I visited a carpenter friend who was building houses and a Mormon church on the Standing Rock Indian Reservation. The two Mormon missionaries were from Hawaii; suffering in the dry heat, they clearly had no idea what the Dakota climate would have in store. For some reason the area was also blanketed that summer by Jehovah's Witnesses, and some Dutch tourists had moved into a haystack near my friend's trailer. They stayed on even after a nearby haystack was hit by lightning.

I prize the hiddenness of Dakota, and have grown protective of the silence here—the places that have become sacred to me, that in all likelihood few humans have ever walked. When I was in Honolulu over Christmas, visiting my family shortly after *Dances With Wolves* came out, I went to parties where I was astonished to hear people discussing South Dakota. "I had no idea it was so lovely," one elegant woman said. "I never thought about South Dakota at all. Now I'd like to see it." *No*, I had to keep myself from saying, *you can't*. Unconscionably, because the state is poor and needs an economic boost, I find myself wanting to keep the professional tourists out.

But tourism is the base of many colonial economies, and the Dakotas have begun to pursue visitors aggressively, offering gambling as a lure. Nearly every storefront along the main street in Deadwood now houses a casino, and the Lower Brule Sioux tribe recently built a giant gambling emporium in eastern South Dakota. More tribes are jumping on the bandwagon; the Midewakanton Sioux operate a casino in neighboring Minnesota with spotlights that come together in the shape of Dakota teepee poles visible in the sky for thirty miles. But this, along with the region's fledgling waste industry, is not particularly good for our self-esteem. Nor is it likely to alter the traditional boom-and-bust economy of the region. And there's always the danger that in selling Dakota to tourists, we'll destroy it. I've lived in Hawaii, after all, and have seen what tourism can do to the soul of a place.

Dakotans know why they like living here, where life is still lived on a human scale. I've banked in New York City and know what a luxury it is to be able to write a counter-check (a blank check on which I write in my own account number) at stores within one hundred miles of home (roughly the distance between New York City and Philadelphia or Los Angeles and Santa Barbara). And small town Dakotans currently have the luxury of a falling crime rate. Of course our population is falling as well, but it can be pleasant to live in a place such as Lemmon, where arrests dropped by a third between 1981 and 1991. Most arrests were made for traffic violations, though we had five burglary arrests in 1985, down to one in 1990 and none in 1991. There have been two murders in the county since I moved there in 1974, and both were family affairs, the killing of old men for their money. It may be odd to think of living in Dakota as a luxury, but I'm well aware that ours is a privileged and endangered way of life, one that, ironically, only the poor may be able to afford. (pp. 33–35)

It seems to us that the narrative form or story of Norris's life in the Dakotas provides a depth, richness, or soul to her writing that would have been missed had she simply described herself with the label from a South Dakota license plate and said "I'm from the state of 'Great Faces And Great Places'" or had she simply provided a statistical description of the population. For instance, in her narrative we heard and could appreciate the "silence" offered by hidden places and, thus, the opportunities they offer for reflecting on the meanings we have created for ourselves. We also saw multiple stories, each with its own impact. We saw stories as presented by the insiders, the Dakotans, and by the outsiders, the "big city" folk and the financiers. Bausch (1991) in describing the characteristics of a story observed that "Individuals, families, and communities also have their identifying stories that link them to who they are, to their culture.... A person without a story is a person with amnesia. A country [or a person] without a story has ceased to exist. A humanity without its story has lost its soul" (p. 33). In the current chapter we have tried to present an approach to family and couple counseling that is based in narrative work and borrows heavily from authors like Michael White and David Epston (Epston & White, 1992; Epston, White, & Murray, 1992; White, 1989a; White, 1995; White & Epston, 1990). This chapter then is divided into three sections and we hope that while making one's way through our comments the reader will reflect on a narrative perspective of clients and counselors as well as a narrative view of the counseling process.

Viewing the Client in a Postmodern World

For the purposes of this chapter, let us imagine a 15-year-old girl named Susan who has been living with her mother, Barbara. We will say that Barbara is a 32-year-old single parent and has never been married, and at the time they entered counseling she was not employed and the family has been living on public assistance. Perhaps as Barbara describes her family situation and her relationship with Susan, she speaks softly and avoids much in the way of eye contact. She complains that as long as she can remember Susan has been unruly at home, and she provides current examples of conflicts that occur when Susan fails to pick up her room, fails to complete washing the dishes after dinner, and forgets to complete her homework. Barbara notes that, like herself, Susan is an only child and Barbara speaks of her own current relationship with her mother that has also become conflictual. She notes that most often her mother criticizes her for issues around her parenting efforts and her current unemployment. Susan also describes the conflict between her and her mother as of concern and acknowledges her mother's view that the conflicts often occur when she doesn't complete chores around home.

Perhaps Barbara and Susan's relationship is explored with a series of circular questions (Nelson, Fleuridas, & Rosenthal, 1986; Selvini Palazzoli, Boscolo, Cecchin, & Prata, 1980; Sanders & Tomm, 1989; Tomm, 1988), for example, "After you forget to clean your room, Susan, how does your mother respond?" "Then, how does your daughter respond to you, Barbara?" and "How does your mother respond to you, Susan?" And perhaps after receiving a description of the mother–daughter relationship, the counselor suggests that Susan and her mother might be able to provide a title for the story that describes their relationship. Barbara may mention that for some time she has been feeling that everything has been becoming increasingly hopeless. Susan, in turn, may think the story in their family could be named "Everything Is Hopeless." This description of the family may seem to capture their sense of hopelessness and later in the initial session Barbara may also agree with the story title.

As suggested by Michael White (1992, 1993a), it would seem that this story title of "Everything Is Hopeless" may have become a frame for the mother and daughter to use in interpreting themselves and their relationship, and it may have seemed that the story suggested to the family that there was indeed little hope for improving their relationship. Along these lines, Brunner (1986, p. 14) noted that the stories that we live can be described according to a "landscape of action" (i.e., our behavior that signals the presence of a particular story) as well as a "landscape of consciousness" (i.e., the meanings these stories hold for ourselves and our relationships). Epston, White, and Murray (1992) also suggested that clients often come to counseling when the stories by which they live appear to be impoverishing, subjugating, or resulting in less than preferred outcomes.

White (1992, 1993a) noted that stories or narratives have real effects in terms of shaping our lives, and so Susan and her mother may have been wishing that things were different between them but all too frequently found themselves reentering nonproductive arguments. White (1992, 1993a) further noted that the stories or narratives by which we live, the "dominant stories" (White & Epston, 1990, p. 41), are constructed through our interactions with others and negotiated with others, and so, Susan and her mother would have been viewed as co-creating a "problem-saturated story" (White & Epston, 1990, p. 16) about "Everything Is Hopeless." That story may have suggested to them that there is no way either of them could alter the conflict in their relationship. White (1992, 1993a) further indicated that these dominant stories, the ones we create about ourselves and our relationships, determine which aspects of our lived experiences we select out for awareness, and so a great deal of our lived experiences fall outside of the dominant story that we have created for ourselves (White & Epston, 1990). Perhaps like some of you who are reading this chapter, we have also heard clients brush aside progress in counseling by noting that "It won't last." Indeed, our ideas about what is real for us and our relationships seem to be a product of our interactions and negotiations with others (Berger & Luckmann, 1966; Gergen, 1991); that is, our realities about ourselves and our relationships can be described as being conversationally created. In the case of Barbara and Susan, they may have had difficulty identifying times when the conflict was not present in their relationship, and if such periods were identified, they may have been discounted or dismissed as not important because they did not fit into the dominant story of "Everything Is Hopeless." Here it is important to remember that the stories in our lives seem to be bound by place and context (Walter, 1988). As a result, the despair felt in the story of "Everything Is Hopeless" may not have been present in other relationships for Barbara in the community or, for that matter, in other relationships Susan had with children from the community. Like many families, they may have been viewed as entering counseling at a particular point in time because the story they were living in their relationship did not provide them with a preferred outcome (Epston, White, & Murray, 1992).

Viewing the Counselor in a Postmodern World

Counselors also have stories about being helpful to the families with whom they work. O'Hanlon and Weiner-Davis (1989) have suggested how the counselor's story about working with a client may help to co-create a client's reality,

> It [the presenting complaint] is shaped by the therapeutic interaction during and after assessment into a more solid "presenting problem." If the client walks into a behaviorist's office, he or she will leave with a behavior problem. If clients choose psychoanalysts' offices, they will leave with unresolved issues from childhood as the focus of the problem. If a client seeks help from a Jungian analyst, he or she is likely to get a problem that can be treated most effectively by examining symbolism in the client's dreams. (p. 54)

The influence of the counselor's story or reality about working with clients has been very real to us, and so we have spent some time considering our own narratives and encouraging students to do the same. For example, a counselor educator, whom we fictitiously refer to as Fran, may now be well into mid-life and reflecting on her own story as a counselor. Perhaps Fran remembers various episodes in the development of this narrative. As a youngster Fran may have found herself struggling to fit in and to find a place in a small town in Illinois. Perhaps the family had moved to this town from Iowa when Fran was quite young while the rest of the extended family remained in the "Hawkeye State." This sense of separateness from the extended family may have played down the importance of connectedness with others and may have served to strengthen a sense of separateness and independence. Part of Fran's narrative or story may have also developed around being only somewhat capable as a student in school. As a result of viewing herself as less than a star-studded student and feeling clumsy at connecting with others, Fran may have become an observer of life. Then perhaps in the 1960s she went off to attend a small college on the plains of South Dakota. On the beautiful open spaces of South Dakota one could stand on the prairie and enjoy a connectedness with the earth and the sky while not feeling pressed by interactions with others. Perhaps parts of this developing story encouraged Fran to become an observer of human behavior and perhaps also pulled her in the direction of studying psychology.

It could be imagined that other parts of Fran's early narrative were formed through relationships with her parents. A strong work ethic may have been one of the family's most prized values, and some of Fran's fondest memories may have revolved around times when family members were all busy with different chores, not necessarily working together, but busy with various responsibilities around the house. As a matter of fact, June to August may have been especially meaningful times that were filled with summer jobs containing various types of responsibilities starting early in the morning. And, of course, many favorable comments may have been heard from neighbors and family members with regard to Fran's work. Indeed, a "Midwestern ethic" that seemed to value work may have formed a foundation for her narrative that perhaps even today guides some of Fran's sense of self and relationships with others. Scenes from Fran's memory of the ocean of green Illinois corn fields planted right up to the road, and farms with lights burning in the barns early in the morning and late at night, might have highlighted a belief about measuring oneself through efforts at being productive.

Then, in college, for one of the first times in Fran's life, we'll imagine that she stumbled into a teacher who actually thought it was possible for Fran to have a story about being a successful student. Perhaps this teacher actually focused on Fran's capabilities as a student and at one point might have even suggested that she consider graduate school. Of course Fran was sure that this teacher did not really know her, because the teacher's story about Fran was somewhat outside her own dominant story about academic proficiency. Perhaps it was not until later in life that Fran started to appreciate the power of stories that were based in competence and possibilities as well as the meaningfulness of narratives that were alternatives to what may have been a problematic and dominant story. But we will say that the relationship with this teacher, his interest in another's capabilities and Fran's view of work, set her on the path to becoming a "scholar" during those undergraduate school days on the South Dakota prairie.

In college this story about the importance of work may at times have been helpful, and later as a graduate student in a counselor education program located in the great Northwest this story may have encouraged Fran to take her studies and clients seriously. What wonderful memories may have remained in the mind's eye of the Northwest, like the high meadows in the Rocky Mountains, where at night one might think it was possible to reach right out and grab the stars. What a terrific place to be young, and the story about being a diligent student might not only have been lived-out while residing in the Northwest but might have also been further formed and supported in Fran's interactions with other graduate students and faculty members. The story might have moved her on to find out the "truth" about clients and the process of counseling as well as the business of education. Perhaps later on, however, Fran would begin to notice how the story had at times limited spontaneity, playfulness, and an ability to develop collaborative relationships. That is, this level of perceived responsibility may at times have left Fran little room for collaborating with others or at times may have left little room for enjoying some of the multiple aspects of life.

From the small town in Illinois to the plains of South Dakota and during part of Fran's time in the Northwest, some of her experiences may have seemed to support notions about free will and individuality as well as the belief about defining herself through work habits. We'll imagine that during graduate school, Fran began her study of the family and perhaps it was not a large stretch for someone from the rural areas of Illinois, South Dakota, and the Northwest to appreciate systemic and interrelated notions of life. The systemic or ecological perspective that was true in nature may have also appeared obvious to her in family systems and other relationships. So there was some challenge to the story about being a counselor who focused on viewing herself and others simply through individual behavior. We'll also suggest that later, on graduating, Fran moved to West Virginia to teach at a small college and while there perceived close ties among some community members and colleagues along the Kanawha and Greenbreier Rivers. These perceptions may have again spoken to her of the systemic nature of things. And then, once more, Fran may have begun to wonder about the interrelatedness of responsibility in relationships and again may have found this to be somewhat freeing in terms of relationships with others.

Another move may have found Fran relocating in the South and joining the faculty at a state university. Perhaps this move once more lifted up the diverse fabric of human existence and called into question systemic nomenclature and highlighted the notion that life consists of multiple stories. For example, perhaps what was perceived as a festive lifestyle of some folks in South Louisiana may have been thought to be in contrast to a more stoic style that perhaps seemed to be expressed by some Midwesterners. Which experience was right, and which would lead to a better life? And, more recently, we will say that Fran relocated to a Northern urban environment where perhaps again the plurality of stories in life has been highlighted. Not only the experiences of being a counselor educator but the delight and challenges of being a parent and spouse, and discussions with others from cultural and gender perspectives different from her own may have produced a curiosity about the plurality of narratives present in our existence. Moreover, the notion of multiple perspectives and realities may have suggested that though any of us can feel stuck at times with a problem-saturated story, unique experiences also exist in which the problematic story is less dominant. An appreciation of these unique experiences and thus alternative stories may have suggested the benefits of reflecting on one's narratives and gaining an appreciation for competencies, resources, and possibilities that are present in life rather than simply trying to understand problems, complaints, and pathologies.

So this realization that there are multiple stories in one's own life and in the lives of others seems to speak to the systemic fabric of existence as well as the opportunities for focusing on narratives that are associated with success and competency. Indeed, this realization would appear to engender a sense of hope in recognizing that realities about ourselves and our relationships are negotiated and created in relationships with others (including counselors) and in recognizing that these constructed realities can contain preferred outcomes for the future.

The Counseling Process in a Postmodern World

Counseling in a postmodern world includes helping clients with the "deconstruction" (White, 1992, pp. 109–151; White, 1993a, pp. 22–61) of those problem-saturated stories that are associated with aspects of a less than preferred life and the "reauthoring" (Epston, White, & Murray, 1992, pp. 96–115; White, 1989c, pp. 5–28) of alternative stories with preferred outcomes (see Figure 1). That is, deconstructing may be useful when clients seem to be so wedded to a problem-saturated story that they may have been unable to see and appreciate those alternative narratives that hold possibilities for them. Thus it follows that deconstructing efforts may not be required with all cases; that is, some clients may more readily view alternative narratives as being part of their lived experiences. Yet in the following remarks we have discussed deconstruction as well as the re-authoring of alternative stories with preferred outcomes. This has been done to provide the reader with a perspective on working with clients who have to a greater extent been claimed by a problem-saturated story. In some ways counseling is an act of listening for sacred, that is, helpful stories and helping clients separate themselves from the profane or problem-saturated stories. Like the writer Scott Russell Sanders (1993) mentioned, counselors help clients "lay out stories to enclose for [themselves] a home ground within the frightening infinities" (p. 193).

Deconstruction

From a postmodern perspective, the counselor views the client as being dominated by a problem-saturated story that results in less than preferred outcomes (Epston, White, & Murray, 1992), and the counselor seeks to help the client consider whether the dominant story is the totality of one's life or the totality of one's relationships with others. White (Bubenzer, West, & Boughner, 1994), in commenting on successful counseling, mentioned

> If the ways of living and thinking that persons often come to therapy with aren't working for them, for whatever reason, I'm interested in

FIGURE 1
Deconstructing and Reauthoring Stories

Deconstructing Problem-Saturated Stories	Reauthoring Alternative Stories
1. Questions to externalize the problem-saturated story	1. Reauthoring by wondering about unique outcomes
2. Comments to normalize a problem-saturated story	2. Reauthoring by wondering about unique accounts
3. Questions to challenge and to wonder how one was recruited into a problem-saturated story	3. Reauthoring by wondering about unique redescriptions
4. Questions that ask the client to become the problem-saturated story	4. Reauthoring by wondering about unique possibilities

> providing a context that contributes to the exploration of other ways of living and thinking. There is always a stock of alternative stories about how life might be, other versions of life as lived. I'm interested in how I might assist persons to step more into those stories that are judged, by them, to be preferred—to perform the alternative understandings or meanings that these stories make possible. (p. 19)

White (1992, 1993a) has described this reconsidering of the dominant and problem-saturated story as a process of deconstruction, and this deconstructing endeavor may be facilitated through a procedure known as "externalizing" (White & Epston 1990, pp. 38–76) of the problem-saturated story. This may be thought of as objectifying the clients' problem-saturated and dominant story in order that the clients might begin to experience the influence of the story on their lives and relationship. For example, imagine that some time ago a single-parent mother (Jane) and her sixteen-year-old daughter (Jennifer) came for counseling. Jane may have been divorced for nine years, and perhaps she noted that for about the past five years she and Jennifer have been involved in an increasing number of arguments. Currently these conflicts may develop around issues like Jennifer not adhering to curfew, Jennifer spending time with friends Jane has not met, and Jane insisting that Jennifer introduce her friends if she wants to spend time with them. Jennifer in turn may complain that her mother wants to know too much about her life, like where she is going and which friends will be with her. They may both agree that the story that would describe their relationship could be titled "A Lack Of Respect." By developing a title for their relationship, the mother and daughter have objectified the problem-saturated story, and this may be helpful in eventually experiencing the influence of the story on their relationship. To assist the clients in experiencing the influence of this story on their relationship, the counselor might ask externalizing questions such as, "How has this story made you feel about yourself as a mother/daughter?" "How has this story required that you respond to each other?" "What habits might I think this story demands of you in order for it to stay present in your relationship?" and "If this story were to dominate your relationship even further, what additional habits might it require of you?" As a result of externalizing the problem-saturated story, White (1993a) noted that

> [clients'] private stories cease to speak to them of their identity and of the truth of their relationships—these private stories are no longer transfixing of persons' lives. Persons experience a separation from, and an alienation in relation to, these stories. In the space

established by this separation, persons are free to explore alternative and preferred knowledges of who they might be, alternative and preferred knowledges into which they might enter their lives. (p. 39)

There are probably many ways of helping clients deconstruct a dominant problem-saturated story. For example, efforts at deconstructing may also include comments that normalize a problem. In working with a single parent who has a story about being "overwhelmed" a counselor might indicate, "I'd be surprised if you didn't feel overwhelmed at times." Or as Tomm (1995) suggested, the counselor might challenge a couple or family members to question certain beliefs (e.g., "How long have you believed in the story of 'Teaching Each Other How To Live'?"). Then the counselor might ask the clients to consider their past and how they were recruited into the problem-saturated story (White, 1992, 1993a, 1993b). For example, the counselor might attempt to help the couple consider how friends, family, or society may have encouraged or supported them in creating the story of "Teaching Each Other How To Live." Perhaps by way of illustration we would find that one or both of the partners were first recruited into this story during childhood when they participated with a parent in criticizing others around a number of issues including skills at being sociable, efforts at work, attempts at parenting and on and on. By suggesting that the clients were recruited into a story that has less than a preferred outcome, the counselor may be implying that other stories may also exist that are descriptive of one's identity or relationships, thus deconstructing the inevitability of the problem-saturated story. Or the counselor might ask the client to become the old and problem-saturated story, and then the counselor might interview this story (the client) around how it knows when the client is most vulnerable to the story, and how the story sneaks into the client's life, and what the client will need to do to continue to make room for this story in one's life (Adams-Westcott et al., 1994). Each time a space is opened for considering an alternative story in one's life or relationships, some deconstructing has taken place. Each time there is an opening of at least a small wedge for a new story about oneself and one's relationships, some deconstructing has occurred.

Reauthoring by Wondering About Unique Outcomes

At moments when the counselor and client have opened this space for a new story about one's self and one's relationships, it is not so much that the counselor is trying to tell the client what story should be lived, but rather the counselor is attempting to help the client consider herself or himself and one's relationships as reflecting a limited narrative, therefore opening the possibility that other stories also exist. As a result, the counselor is interested in helping clients identify experiences, landscape of action events in their lives that have alternative and preferred outcomes (e.g., times when children and parents have not found themselves in conflict or times when partners have been able to offer one another support). Again, Epston, White, and Murray (1992, pp. 96–115) and White (1989c, pp. 5–28) have referred to this process as helping the client with "re-authoring" of her or his life. In order to identify these preferred outcomes in clients' lives, the counselor poses questions to clients that White and Epston (1990) termed "relative influence questions" (pp. 42–48) or other questions that White (1989b) has referred to as "unique outcome questions" (pp. 41–42). Here the counselor is attempting to find out when the client was able to defeat the dominant problem-saturated story. White and Epston (1990) have suggested that a counselor's questions can be designed to recruit knowledge that is an alternative to the problem-saturated story.

A cautionary note needs to be raised, however. Our experience suggests that it seems necessary for the counselor to continually demonstrate a respectful appreciation for the discomfort and pain the dominant problem-saturated story has generated. Rushing quickly into a search for unique outcomes may signal to the client that one's concerns are being trivialized. This appreciation for the client's life needs to continue throughout counseling, and in part, this respect for the problem-saturated story may occur as the counselor and client externalize the dominant story and consider how it has subjugated the client. At some point, however, the counselor may start to wonder about outcomes and experiences that are unique or outside the realm of the dominant problem-saturated story by posing what O'Hanlon and Weiner-Davis (1989, pp. 79–81) have referred to as "presuppositional questions" (e.g., "When have you found yourself defeating this old story?" or "When have you found your relationship being less tyrannized by this old story?"). This type of an open-ended question presupposes that unique events or outcomes have taken place or are taking place. A piece of the assumption here is that change is continually taking place, which differs from the notion that clients' lives are stuck or stalled in a pathogenic pattern. These presuppositional questions seem similar to those designed by de Shazer (1988, pp. 131–151) and seem to look for "exceptions" to the problem. White (1989b, p. 41) noted that such questions may also be phrased in an "indirect" manner (e.g., "When might your parents have thought you were making an effort to defeat that old story?"). Indirect questions appear to place an additional distance between the clients and their old story and, therefore, seem to facilitate clients' efforts at identifying unique outcomes. Zimmerman and Dickerson (1993) highlighted an important consideration in the narrative perspective by mentioning that the importance of unique outcomes resides in the fact that they become opportunities for considering alternative stories about clients and their relationships. And so, at some point, the counselor will attempt to also explore with clients what new meanings can be suggested from the unique outcomes.

White and Epston (1990) and White (1995) have proposed that between sessions the counselor might consider trying to stay involved in the client's life through letter writing. They noted these letters to be meaningful to some clients, and our experience also suggests that a thoughtful letter can open an opportunity for reflection. For example, the counselor might recount in a letter the influence of the dominant story on the client or on the client's relationships with others. The counselor might then conclude the brief letter by wondering about unique outcomes when the client made an effort to defeat or sidestep the dominant problem-saturated story, and mention that she or he will look forward to seeing the client at the next appointment and hearing about those times when the client was not defeated by the problem-saturated story. The following illustrates such a letter:

> Dear Richard and Tom:
>
> This letter is being written as a follow-up to our session. You helped me gain some understanding of how the story about the "Never Ending Conflict" has affected both of you as well as your relationship with each other. Richard, in part, it seemed that you thought the "Never Ending Conflict" had robbed you of something.
>
> That something appeared to be a better relationship with your son, Tom. Tom, you also suggested that the "Never Ending Conflict" had robbed you of a better relationship with your father.
>
> Although you reported that the story about the "Never Ending Conflict" seemed never ending at times, I found it interesting that you could remember a time when it wasn't so strong and influential. You both talked about a time when you enjoyed bike trips together and you seemed to suggest that this was a time when the "Never Ending Conflict" wasn't as successful at imposing its will on you. I also wondered about other occasions when you kept the "Never Ending Conflict" from disrupting your relationship. At our next meet-

ing we might spend some time talking about occasions when you made an effort to prevent "Never Ending Conflict" from imposing itself on you.

Sincerely,

White (1989c) also noted that unique outcomes can have a future focus, and the counselor might wonder about "future unique outcomes" (p. 19). At times, for instance, clients may have difficulty identifying outcomes from their recent or distant past that are unique to the problem-saturated story and the counselor might inquire, "If things were different and this old story wasn't so dominant, how would you like to see your relationship in the future?" or "If you were feeling better about your relationship and not being dominated by the old story, what would you be doing differently?" or "If you could undo how you responded to your father last week, how would you choose to respond to him next time when you find yourself being influenced by the old story?" These questions have some similarity to de Shazer's (1988) "miracle question" (pp. 5–6). It is also possible that unique outcomes will "present themselves in the course of the session" (White, 1989c, p.18) and here the counselor might share such an observation during the course of a session when clients are not cooperating with the problem- saturated story. For example, perhaps the clients make an attempt to be supportive of each other, or to listen to one another, or to simply refrain from being critical, and the counselor could then point to this as being unique or different from the dominant story. White (1989c) referred to these as "current unique outcomes" (pp. 18–19), but whether the counselor is focusing on current or future unique outcomes, one will want to add some substance and context to these events by inquiring about what has accounted for them.

Reauthoring by Wondering About Unique Accounts

To facilitate a sense of hope and agency, the counselor is interested in helping clients lift up and identify events that are unique or different from the old problem-saturated story (e.g., times when Richard and Tom would have ordinarily succumbed to an old story of "Never Ending Conflict" and either side-stepped the dominance of the old story or made progress in loosening the grip of the old story on their relationship). By inquiring about a string of unique outcomes, the counselor can "thicken the plot" (White, 1993b) of an emerging alternative story. As part of this effort the counselor might ask, "How did you prepare yourself for this effort to loosen the grip of the old story on your relationship?" or "What did you notice yourself doing differently when you were making an effort to defeat the old story?" or "What would your son have reported you did to side-step the old story?" White (1989b) has referred to these questions as "unique account questions" (pp. 42–43), and it is not unusual that after exploring a series of unique outcomes and accounts that an alternative story can be identified. This may be identified by asking the clients what new story these new events suggest, or by the counselor suggesting a new story title that has occurred to her or him and then presenting it for the clients' consideration. Obviously, this very much talks to a process of co-creating or co-authoring an alternative story with clients where preferred outcomes are realized.

Of course family members may present with problem-saturated stories that are descriptive of relationships in the family, or in some cases a story may be more meaningful for one member of the family. That is, stories exist for individuals as well as for relationships, and as previously noted, they function to guide our lived experiences. For instance, for Susan, the young girl mentioned at the beginning of this chapter, a new story of "Feeling More Hopeful When Everyone Is Respected" could have emerged and could have been seen as meaningful. It may have been that although her mother attended the counseling sessions, much of the conversation may have moved between Susan and the counselor. Perhaps toward the end of counseling, Susan's mother would have mentioned that her relationship with her daughter was changing and perhaps she would have talked about being less controlling with Susan. It has seemed to occur on occasion that when a new story of competence was developing for a young person, a parent appeared to deconstruct an old and problematic story about himself or herself as a failing parent and to replace it with a story of competence as they saw their child identifying with an alternative story.

If the counselor thought it appropriate, she or he could write a letter to clients who are trying to identify unique accounts. This may also facilitate efforts to identify a story that is an alternative to the dominant and problem-saturated story. The counselor, for example, might think it helpful to recount times when the client or clients were able to identify themselves or their relationship as being less subjugated by the problem-saturated story and then ask what the client did or thought to bring about those unique outcomes. By inquiring about unique accounts, clients are being asked to give further thought to times when the problem-saturated story had not been so dominant, and the counselor might conclude the letter by asking for consideration of an alternative story title for one's life or relationships. The following might act as an illustration of such a letter:

Dear Richard and Tom:

It was good to see you last week. After our appointment I once more found myself thinking of you. Again I was struck by the times you mentioned when you prevented the "Never Ending Conflict" from being so strong and influential in your relationship. You both noted times when you enjoyed bike trips together and times when you enjoyed taking walks together in the evening. I found myself wondering what each of you had done to bring about those special moments. How did you make these special moments happen? And I was struck by the thought that these special times (and your efforts to bring them about) indicated another story in your relationship, one that is more hopeful and different from the story about "Never Ending Conflict." I was curious as to what you would call this new story. What would be a good name for this new story? Perhaps at our next appointment we can discuss these questions.

Sincerely,

Reauthoring by Wondering About Unique Redescriptions

White (1989b) has also noted that the reauthoring process can be facilitated by inquiry into what the new story says to a client about oneself or relationships with others, and he has referred to these as "unique redescription questions" (pp. 43–44). These questions inquire into the client's landscape of consciousness (meaning); that is, the significance one attributes to the place of the new story in one's life. For example, one couple may enter counseling with an old story about a "Lack of Consideration for Each Other." After identifying times when each experienced some level of consideration from the other and after identifying an alternative story about "Considering Each Other" the couple might be asked, "What does the new story about 'Considering Each Other' say to you about your relationship?" or "What does this new story say to your partner about who you are in this relationship?" It is not unusual for family members to note that the new story has generated a meaning for their relationship that includes an increased sense of hope for the relationship.

Letters to clients pertaining to a redescription of meaning might begin by recounting the influence of the old story in the clients' relationship and then contrasting this by wondering about the meaning of the alternative story in their relationship. To further help clients reflect on the meaningfulness of the alternative story, the counselor might ask clients to consider what the new story says to them about themselves or their relationships. A brief letter like this might be concluded by suggesting that the counselor would be interested in hearing from the clients about new meanings the alternative story has for them. The following illustration exemplifies these ideas:

> Dear Richard and Tom:
>
> I was thinking about seeing you next week and remembering our last meeting together. At our last appointment you discussed two stories that described your father–son relationship; one story of "Never Ending Conflict" and an alternative story about "Viewing Each Other As Important." Richard mentioned living the alternative story when he reminded himself to listen to events in Tom's life during evening walks. Tom mentioned living the alternative story when he considered his dad's suggestions in preparing for a bike trip.
>
> At our next appointment I thought it might be interesting to explore what living the alternative story about "Viewing Each Other As Important" says about your father–son relationship.
>
> Sincerely,

White (1993b) also noted that clients may be asked to evaluate which of their stories, the old or new, would lead to a preferred outcome and therefore to indicate which would be the preferred narrative. It has seemed to us that this question inquires into the clients' landscape of consciousness or meaning, particularly when the counselor follows up by asking why the clients prefer either the old or new story. New meanings about oneself and one's relationships with others are generated from the new and alternative story, and these new meanings can be viewed as being recursively related or interwoven with new behaviors in the landscape of action.

Reauthoring by Wondering About Unique Possibilities

The more one sees one's life as having a specific and certain meaning connected with her or his existence, the more likely it is that one's behavior becomes congruent with these beliefs. Likewise, one's behavior is likely to confirm beliefs one holds about self and relationships with others. As a result and as part of the reauthoring process, White (1989b) also wrote of "unique possibility questions" (pp. 44–45). Here the intent is to help clients consider their futures as individuals as well as the future of their relationships, and consequently, the focus is on the next steps in implementing a new story in one's life and relationships. So for example, during a family counseling session the counselor may find herself or himself asking questions like, "If you were to think further about letting this new story of 'Considering Each Other' into your life, what would be your next step?" or "If you found the old story sneaking back into your relationship, how could this new story get you back on track again?" or "Knowing what I know about you, what might I think would be your next step in living this new story?"

If the counselor wanted to stay in touch with clients between appointments, he or she could write a letter that focuses on possibilities for further implementing the new story. After reflecting on the clients' perceptions of the new story in their life, the counselor could ask them to consider what they might do to further live the new story. To consider this procedure, the reader might take a look at the following illustration:

> Dear Richard and Tom:
>
> As you know, sometimes after seeing people I find myself thinking about one or more of our meetings, and I'd like to share some of these thoughts and questions with you. At our last meeting I was touched by the meanings you found in the alternative story about "Viewing Each Other As Important." Richard's comments about how the alternative story encouraged him to present a view of being respectful of others seemed meaningful, and Tom's comments about the alternative story generating respect from others as a result of seeing them as important suggested an ability to form strong relationships. At this point I've also found myself wondering where this alternative story of "Viewing Each Other As Important" might lead you as father and son; that is, what does the new story suggest as a direction for you in the next couple of weeks? I would be interested in exploring this direction with you at our next meeting and will look forward to seeing you then.
>
> Sincerely,

White (1992, 1993a) and White and Epston (1990) have noted that a certain realness is infused into narratives as people begin to live alternative stories and as the new stories are witnessed by others. White (Bubenzer, West, & Boughner, 1994) has mentioned, "So, regardless as to whether I am meeting with an individual, a couple, or a family, I am thinking about possible audiences to the unfolding developments of therapy, and thinking about how this audience might be invited to play a part in the authentication of the preferred claims that are emerging in the process of the therapy" (pp. 26–27). Thus he has talked about having clients recruit an audience into witnessing the emergence of a new story and discusses with them how to introduce others to the new story in their lives. It seems that Gilligan (1993) was also speaking to this process when he mentioned that "Witnesses not only observe a person's declarations but also participate in and validate the creation of a new social and psychological identity" (p. 248). For example, a couple may have a story about "Disappointment With Our Relationship." This story may have been reported to have been evident when requests were ignored, when one made plans without consulting the other partner, and when one chose to spend time with others (friends and relatives) without inviting the partner. This narrative may have been making it difficult for the couple to appreciate much about their relationship. An alternative story ("Being Proud Of Our Relationship") may have provided the couple with pleasure after considering each other's requests, may have informed the couple of the value in consulting with one another before making plans, and may have suggested a joy gathered from time spent together. In order to recruit an audience to support a new story, White (1992, 1993a) has suggested asking clients to identify who might be an appropriate audience for their new story, asking clients to discuss how they might introduce the new story to these persons, and asking clients to discuss how they might invite the audience to respond to the new story. So for example, the counselor might ask, "Who from your past or present (family/friends/colleagues) would be likely to see this new story entering your relationship?" "What might you do to make them aware of the importance of this new story in your relationship?" "How do you suppose you might find out about their reaction to this new story in your relationship?"

In a similar manner, Freedman and Combs (1996) suggested that the counselor might help the clients assemble a team of people who could be used to support an alternative story. For instance, the counselor could ask, "Who might support this new story in your relationship?" Because the counselor is trying to help the clients identify a team, this question could be asked again and so the audience might include more than a couple of individuals, "And who else might support this new story?" These clients might or might not ever discuss their counseling or their new story with the audience (team), but the audience can become important to the therapeutic process and important to anchoring a new story when the counselor asks the clients to consider possible responses the audience might make to questions like, "What might your sister say this new story says about your relationship?" "What might your grandfather say is the next step in living this new story?" "What might your friend suggest as a way to start reliving your new story after the disappointment of this past week?" During continued counseling, the team members can remain important when the counselor asks clients what team members would suggest with regard to supporting the new story: "Which members of the team would understand this setback?" "How would those team members suggest that you might start living the new story again?" "Which team members would have thoughts on how your success of the past week fits with the new story of your relationship and what would they say?" It has seemed to us that generating audiences can have an important place in the development of new stories and White's (1993a) comments would also seem to provide a rationale in support of this therapeutic practice: "ordinarily persons achieve a sense of authenticity when (a) they perform particular claims about their lives, claims that relate to particular self-narratives, and when (b) this performance is witnessed by themselves and/or others" (p. 25). Indeed, because we as human beings are social animals, the witnessing by others of our stories about ourselves and our relationships supports their authenticity.

Conclusion

This chapter seems to us to be an example of the "text analogy" (White & Epston, 1990, pp. 9–13) at work. We would not hold our comments out as "narrative counseling" but rather as our construction of the narrative counseling process that has been informed by our experiences with families and colleagues and students, and our understandings of what we perceive to be some very stimulating reading. After reviewing our initial considerations of narrative counseling, interested readers are certainly encouraged to continue their own reading in this area and to consider the works listed in the reference section of this chapter. Moreover, because this perspective seems to present us with a unique process of languaging about our work as counselors (e.g., considering the multiplicity of embedded stories in life and relationships), we suggest that counselors interested in working from this paradigm consider receiving supervision in order to become more fully acquainted with the narrative position.

As White (Bubenzer, West, & Boughner, 1994) has suggested, it needs to be kept in mind that the process of narrative counseling does not necessarily travel a linear path from (a) deconstruction to (b) creating unique outcomes and accounts and then (c) on to redescriptions of a new story and (d) to considering opportunities associated with the new story. Unlike the manner in which our comments on narrative counseling are laid out, counselor and client conversations are actually much more varied in nature. For example, counselors and clients might find themselves weaving in and around the deconstruction of old stories, through the considering of unique outcomes and accounts, and back again to further deconstruct an old story, and on to naming a new story while also considering new possibilities, and then perhaps further deconstructing an old story and then reflecting on the meaning of the new story in one's life and relationships, and so on and so on. Perhaps the reader will view this type of counseling process as resonating more closely with the business of life and as being sensitive to the responses and directions provided by clients.

References

Adams-Westcott, J., Combs, G., Dickerson, V., Freedman, J., Neal, J., & Zimmermann, J. (1994, November). *Narrative therapy and supervision: A postmodern experience.* Paper presented at the American Association for Marriage and Family Therapy Conference, Chicago, IL.

Bausch, W. J. (1991). *Storytelling: Imagination and faith.* Mystic, CT: Twenty-Third Publications.

Berger, P. L., & Luckmann, T. (1966). *The Social construction of reality: A treatise in the sociology of knowledge.* New York: Doubleday.

Brunner, J. (1986). *Actual minds, possible worlds.* Cambridge, MA: Harvard University Press.

Bubenzer, D. L., West, J. D., & Boughner, S. R. (1994). Michael White and the narrative perspective in therapy. *The Family Journal: Counseling and Therapy for Couples and Families, 2,* 71–83.

de Shazer, S. (1988). *Investigating solutions in brief therapy.* New York: Norton.

Epston, D., & White, M. (1992). *Experience, contradiction, narrative and imagination: Selected papers of David Epston and Michael White 1989–1991.* Adelaide, South Australia: Dulwich Centre Publications.

Epston, D., White, M., & Murray, K. (1992). A proposal for a re-authoring therapy: Rose's revisioning of her life and a commentary. In S. McNamee & K. J. Gergen (Eds.), *Therapy as social construction* (pp. 96–115). London: Sage.

Freedman, J., & Combs, G. (1996). *Narrative therapy: The social construction of preferred realities.* New York: Norton.

Gergen, K. J. (1991). *The saturated self: Dilemmas of identity in contemporary life.* New York: Basic Books.

Gilligan, S. (1993). Therapeutic rituals: Passages into new identities. In S. Gilligan & R. Price (Eds.), *Therapeutic conversations* (pp. 237–257). New York: Norton.

Nelson, T. S., Fleuridas, C., & Rosenthal, D. M. (1986). The evaluation of circular questions: Training family therapists. *Journal of Marital and Family Therapy, 12*, 113–127.

Norris, K. (1993). *Dakota: A spiritual geography.* New York: Ticknor & Fields.

O'Hanlon, W. H., & Weiner-Davis, M. (1989). *In search of solutions: A new direction in psychotherapy.* New York: Norton.

Sanders, S. R. (1993). *Staying put: Making a home in a restless world.* Boston: Beacon Press.

Sanders, G., & Tomm, K. (1989). A cybernetic-systemic approach to problems in sexual functioning. In D. Kentor & B. F. Okun (Eds.), *Intimate environments: Sex, intimacy, and gender in families* (pp. 346–380). New York: Guilford Press.

Selvini Palazzoli, M., Boscolo, L., Cecchin, G., & Prata, G. (1980). Hypothesizing-circularity-neutrality: Three guidelines for the conductor of the session. *Family Process, 19*, 3–12.

Tomm, K. (1988). Interventive interviewing: Part III. Intending to ask lineal, circular, strategic, or reflexive questions. *Family Process, 27*, 1–15.

Tomm, K. (1995, September). *Co-constructing therapeutic realities in systemic family therapy.* Presentation sponsored by Akron Child Guidance Center and the International Family Therapy Training Institute, Akron, OH.

Walter, E. V. (1988). *Placeways: A theory of the human environment.* Chapel Hill, NC: University of North Carolina Press.

White, M. (1989a). *Selected papers.* Adelaide, South Australia: Dulwich Centre Publications.

White, M. (1989b). The process of questioning: A therapy of literary merit? In M. White (Ed.), *Selected papers* (pp. 37–46). Adelaide, South Australia: Dulwich Centre Publications.

White, M. (1989c). The externalizing of the problem and the re-authoring of lives and relationships. In M. White (Ed.), *Selected papers* (pp. 5–28). Adelaide, South Australia: Dulwich Centre Publications.

White, M. (1992). Deconstruction and therapy. In D. Epston & M. White (Eds.), *Experience, narrative and imagination: Selected papers of David Epston and Michael White 1989–1991* (pp. 109–151). Adelaide, South Australia: Dulwich Centre Publications.

White, M. (1993a). Deconstruction and therapy. In S. Gilligan & R. Price (Eds.), *Therapeutic conversations* (pp. 22–61). New York: Norton.

White, M. (1993b, October). *The narrative metaphor and collaborative therapy.* Paper presented at the 5th Annual National Workshop On Family Therapy sponsored by the Hannah Neil Institute and the Starr Institute, Columbus, OH.

White, M. (1995). *Re-authoring lives: Interviews and essays.* Adelaide, South Australia: Dulwich Centre Publications.

White, M., & Epston, D. (1990). *Narrative means to therapeutic ends.* New York: Norton.

Zimmerman, J. L., & Dickerson, V. C. (1993). Bringing forth the restraining influence of pattern in couples therapy. In S. Gilligan & R. Price (Eds.), *Therapeutic conversations* (pp. 197–214). New York: Norton.

■ ■ ■

4

The Reflecting Position: Theoretical, Counselor, and Client Perspectives

John J. Zarski, PhD
Alan L. Sterling, MD
Patricia E. Parr, PhD

In this chapter the authors introduce the idea of the reflecting position to counseling, provide guidelines for its use in treatment, discuss the counselor's role in a postmodern world, examine the counselor's relationship with the reflecting team, explore the impact of the reflecting team on counselor education, and conclude with a section on client responses to the reflecting position in counseling.

Beginning with Gregory Bateson's pioneering efforts applying cybernetic theory to human interactions (Bateson, 1951; Bateson, Jackson, Haley, & Weakland, 1956; Guttman, 1991), revolutionary ideas have evolved that question the Western modern scientific structural view of the world. Previous theories have been based on the structural concept that specific truths or realities exist and are represented by and, thus, are discoverable through words or language (de Shazer, 1994).

One of the most revolutionary theories is the concept of constructivism (von Glasersfeld, 1984), which employs the idea of cybernetic feedback loops to imply that there is no one reality, but rather that realities are constructed based on a person's interaction with the environment. In other words, feedback loops are the circular mechanisms by which information from a person's interaction with the environment is reintroduced to the person initiating a further chain of subsequent events.

More recently, refinements of constructivistic ideas have evolved (Gergen, 1985; Hoffman, 1988). As opposed to constructivism, these approaches pay specific attention to intersubjective loops of dialogue and not to cybernetic feedback loops (Hoffman, 1991). In social constructionistic thinking, concepts, meanings, and memories arise out of social interaction and are mediated through language. Indeed, social constructionism is diachronic and the social interactors can co-create distinctions, explanations, and meanings from moment to moment out of the interactors' existing but constantly changing knowledge-experiential, structurally determined base (Maturana & Varela, 1992).

Therapeutic approaches in this list of refinements include the narrative (White & Epston, 1990); solution-oriented (Walter & Peller, 1992); temporal diachronic (Boscolo & Bertrando, 1993); and the reflective position (Andersen, 1991). Tom Andersen's reflecting position, as much as any, exemplifies the mutually shared position of interactive responsibility for meanings and understandings. In terms of counseling, this implies that novel concepts and meaning (i.e., alternative realities), can be created by means of the social interactive mechanism of dialogue or, in plain English, conversation.

In introducing the idea of reflecting, Andersen builds on three primary concepts. These are structural determinism (Maturana & Varela, 1992), "the difference that makes a difference" (Bateson, 1972), or in Andersen's words, "the appropriately unusual," and conversation as the means of exchange of ideas (Andersen, 1991).

Structural determinism is primary to Andersen's way of thinking. As part of this concept Maturana and Varela (1992) implied that at any certain point in time one can only perceive and therefore react and interact in ways that one's repertoire of knowledge and experience allows. Because perceptions are observer-based realities and every observer has a different repertoire, there are multiple possible perceptions or realities of any observed event. Thus, as perceptions lead to distinctions, explanations, and then meanings, an indeterminate number of possible realities can be co-created.

The way into this repertoire is through conversation. Conversations within one's own head, that is self-talk (Tomm, 1988), may have a profound effect on making distinctions and connections but are limited to the perceptions that come out of one's own repertoire and thus are self-limiting and often entrenching. Conversations with others, on the other hand, allow for consideration of descriptions and explanations that come from others' perceptions and have the possibility of opening up space (Tomm, 1988). Open space implies that other options or differences can be entertained and can lead to new distinctions, descriptions, and explanations that lead to an enhanced repertoire. Because the repertoire is built out of one's history, biases, beliefs, experiences, and knowledge these too change as space is opened up.

When differences that could possibly make a difference are entertained, usually through exchange via dialogue, they must not be so strange as to be discarded as a foreign object, yet at the same time they must be different enough to spark new connections or new distinctions. That is to say that they must be "appropriately unusual." Andersen (1991) wrote that he is always in search of the appropriately unusual, which nearly always is a search for the unknown.

Conversations then are the important source for the exchange of the appropriately unusual. It is these exchanges that recolor old descriptions and lead to new distinctions. Attitudes and behaviors change according to the alternatives that are co created and the optional narratives (White & Epston, 1990) that can be entertained.

Maturana and Varela (1992) premise the concept of structural determinism on the biologic-physiologic-anatomic given (i.e., the structure of each organism). In regard to perceptions, the sensory-cerebral structure of each individual has a potential and cannot go beyond that potential until the structure changes. The structure, however, being constantly affected by the environment, is in a dynamic state.

Paraphrasing Andersen (1987), the goal of reflecting is to promote second order change; that is, fundamental changes in a system's organization and function. This is in contrast to a first level change, which is change within a system that does not alter the basic organization of the system itself. The reflecting position advances second order change by engaging in dialogue in order to understand how the various persons came to create their descriptions and explanations and then to invite them into a conversation that allows the existence of not yet seen or thought of descriptions and explanations. These novel descriptions and explanations then can become knowledge or alternatives that prime the system for finding further new meanings that promote alternative interactions and attitudes. In effect, this is second level change as it implies not only that a problem may be solved but also that the repertoire has expanded in such a way that new coping is resultant from new meanings.

Although the concept of the reflecting team is associated with Andersen (1991) as the specific modality of counseling or consultative interaction, it is actually conversation as Andersen defines it that promotes the possibility of opening up space. Conversation, as a series of questions that may be expressed as thoughts, ideas, or fantasies, provides the fodder for possible change. Although a reflecting team, through its multiple voices, may generate the greatest amount of novel descriptions and explanations, it is just one way to entertain such reflective conversation. These conversations or reflectings also can take place in many other ways. These include conversations between a counselor and family or individual, or between a collaborator or consultant and a therapeutic system directly, or between multiple consultants or reflectors and the therapeutic system.

Guidelines for the Reflecting Position

In actuality, a reflecting team is not a therapeutic modality but is a formalized methodology for providing a type of conversation (reflecting) that may open up space by entertaining previously unthought of alternatives. A team is not necessary for this type of conversation to take place, and it is important to note that Andersen devotes a significant section of his book, *The Reflecting Team* (1991), to the use of therapeutic conversation without a team. In addition, there are many ways a reflecting team can be constructed. The team can enter into conversation at any time a team member may have a thought or idea that may be helpful. Also the team may remain in the room with the therapeutic system or may use a one-way mirror for observing. If a one-way mirror is used, the reflecting team and the therapeutic system exchange observing postures either by changing rooms or by flipping the lights on for those in the conversational position and off for those in the listening position.

At the Akron Child Guidance Center, where the coauthors have worked on projects related to reflective conversation, a one-way mirror is frequently used. As Andersen (1991) suggested, the reflecting team first observes the therapeutic system in conversation, then the therapeutic system observes the reflecting team's conversation and the distinctions they make regarding the therapeutic system, and then finally the reflecting team listens to and observes the therapeutic system as they consider the team's reflections.

In terms of mechanics, the process takes place as follows:

1. During the course of events at the Child Guidance Center, a counselor identifies a need for the therapeutic system to be referred for a reflecting team consultation. Often this is because the therapeutic system appears to be stuck. A time is set, usually a two-hour block of time that is routinely kept available for such purposes, and the family is invited to attend.
2. Before the family is interviewed by the counselor, a brief discussion takes place with the counselor, the counselor's supervisor, the consulting (reflecting) team, and the other professional attendees. This conversation is limited in scope so that only descriptive information about the family, the current developments in the therapeutic process, the reason the family has been referred, and the expectations of the counselor are clarified. Specifically, new ideas, beliefs, alternatives, curiosity inquiries, or cause and effect or circular explanations are not entertained or at least not divulged. The specific reasons for these limits will be discussed later.
3. Those observing, everybody other than the stuck system, go behind the mirror and the family is invited into the family therapy room. The family, which has been previously prepared by the counselor for the observational process, is then reintroduced to the purpose and expected plan of events and is asked if they would like to see the observation room or meet the reflecting team members before the conversation between the counselor and family members begins.
4. The interview between the counselor and the other members of the stuck system then proceeds. The therapeutic system works together for about 30 to 40 minutes, following which the observing team and stuck system exchange places. Up until this point, silence is pretty much maintained in the viewing room, however, on occasion the supervisor might find it necessary to intervene. For example, the supervisor might enter the room to redirect the therapist to speak to other members of the therapeutic system.
5. The observing team then reflects for about 5 to 15 minutes, after which the observers and the therapeutic system again switch places. The observing team's reflections focus on describing a

client's strengths, what the client is doing to solve problems, and phrases or metaphors used by the client. Team members use indirect statements or questions (e.g., "I wonder . . .," or "What will happen if. . . ,") as ways to provide alternate views of the situations. After this second switch, the family members, at the prompting of the counselor, exchange ideas and observations about the reflecting process and what they heard that may be affirming or useful to them, and they may discuss briefly any new or additional ideas or thoughts that have evolved in the course of the process. This may go rather quickly, lasting only 5 or 10 minutes, or on occasion up to about 20 minutes if the therapeutic system seems to be in a generative conversation.

6. Finally, the family leaves and a postsession takes place with the observers (reflecting team), the counselor, and the supervisor. This may last about 10 to 15 minutes, but with some frequency lasts 30 minutes as this conversing often promotes discussion as new ideas and thoughts evolve and alternative possible reflections are discussed. We often purposely look for "all the other" possible perceptions that could have occurred to the reflectors.
7. Occasionally, we will conduct a follow-up with the therapeutic system. These follow-ups may be initiated by either member of the therapeutic system (counselor or client). Because associations of thought and action often process over time and are sparked by unpredictable happenings in life or through therapy encounters, we have found that follow-ups are best arranged between one and three months following the initial meeting.

We use the described methodology because it is a fairly simple and easily defined framework, but hold to it in its purest form only if research or study protocol requires such adherence. Otherwise we are quite free to change or alter the flow for the sake of conversation or reflecting that may open up space or might be generative. For example, on occasion and at any point during the family interview process, an observer might entertain a novel idea or alternative that would best be expressed in a timely fashion. In such a case, the observer may take the reflecting posture, go into the interview room, and enter the therapeutic system's conversation.

Although conversation and co-creating is the key to reflecting, such conversation is saved for times when the team converses or for the times when an observer becomes a reflector and enters the therapeutic system. Dialogue is purposely avoided by the team in the presession and while observing so that each observer is free to think independently, thus enabling as many perceptions as possible to be stimulated by the flow of the therapeutic system's discourse and actions. Otherwise, when professional observers share ideas during the observing, they tend to limit their creativity by focusing on each other's ideas, often forming a more or less common theme. Indeed, many counselors are well practiced in collaborating in such a way that as a group they easily derive a particular point of view, plan, or intervention that excludes alternatives and limits creativity.

Because the therapeutic system can be easily overwhelmed by too many new ideas, usually we have three and sometimes four persons carry on a reflecting conversation. This is true even if there are multiple observers present. In such a case, we wait until shortly before it is time to change places to decide who the reflectors will be. This decision is somewhat spontaneous, depending on who feels that they have some thoughts or inclinations they would like to put into the open. Should the occasion arise that not enough of the observers are so energized, some observers are gently volunteered by the group. Interestingly enough, between the time they are volunteered and the time the conversation takes place, they come up with thoughts or curiosities or descriptions that often are the most stimulating and possibly helpful.

The primary reason for using three or four reflectors is that this seems to be the right number in most cases to allow enough generation of ideas so multiple novel perceptions can be exchanged, but at the same time it is not so many that the family is so overwhelmed that they lose interest or focus. It is important that they have the opportunity to carry away some meaningful options. In this regard, we attempt to limit the length of the reflecting conversation even though the reflectors are encouraged to respond in conversation to each other. Each reflector usually verbalizes two or three thoughts either stimulated by the previous observing or by the current conversation.

Finally, the way one converses in front of or with the therapeutic system is exceedingly important. If possible the family's "language" is employed. Also, the reflectors maintain a normative, nonjudgmental, but interested and curious posture often looking to strengths and positive outlooks. Above all, descriptions or inferences about family members or their interactions are positively connoted (Andersen, 1991).

In addition, the conversation should be styled so that the talk is not conclusive of any point of view or idea. The family must be free to pick and choose and relate to any material without a sense of obligation or coercion. These thoughts are presented in such a way that the reflectors show no investment in them so the family can readily discard them. To accomplish this, phrases such as "The thought just hit me. . .," "I'm not sure if this even pertains, but. . .," "I had this fantasy. . .," "That could be, but I'm wondering if. . .," or "The question keeps coming back to me, 'What if . . .?'" are frequently used.

Overall, the effect of such reflecting or conversation is meant to be empowering. New connections, new possibilities, and new perceptions that are curious and future oriented are at least energizing if not immediately fully embraced. Additionally, the sense of involvement as an "equal" in a collaborative process with trained professionals promotes a keen interest in the process as well as confirmation of the family and the therapeutic system as capable of progress.

It is interesting to note just how involved the family becomes in the process and how affectively they change during the process. This may be attributable to the effects of being able to "eavesdrop," but nevertheless the family members become "glued to the glass" once they enter the observation room and the conversation begins. "Depressed" persons sit up and listen and even "hyperactive" kids freeze for periods of time and look and listen. It is not unusual for individuals to tear up, and they usually say that they are tears of "feeling understood." Then almost without fail, once the family is resituated in the therapy room following the reflecting team's conversation, they appear different, sometimes dramatically. They may sit in different places (even though for every therapy session up until then, they always took the same positions), sit with different postures, show different affect, or speak in a different manner. If little else, they frequently say that they are amazed that "they really seemed to know us in a short period of time."

The postsessions of observers and professionals are also of great interest. Further ideas and connections are usually entertained. These are related both to the family and to the professional's approach and planning. Counselors almost always believe that new options and insights are created. Supervisors, too, usually feel that they have some viable alternatives with which to be helpful.

However, whatever the immediate changes may be, it is of course the maintenance of these changes or the occurrence of future changes (*seeding of the unconscious* to use a Carl Whitaker [1975] term) or coping that is most crucial. It needs to be kept in mind that, while most clinicians who use reflecting contend that reflecting team conversations are useful both in the short and long term, the only definitive evidence of such is related to the family referencing it, and even this could be incidental. In his book, *The Reflecting Team* (1991), Andersen gives a number of case examples that show the efficacy of the reflecting team over time following the initial consultation.

The Counselor in a Postmodern World

The late 1980s and early 1990s marked a period of enormous change in the field of counseling. As pointed out in the previous section, new and exciting ideas have challenged both counselors and clients relative to their respective perspectives on the process and outcome of counseling. In this section we will discuss the counselor's role when operating from a social constructionist framework, the relationship between the counselor and the reflecting team in a postmodern world, and then conclude with some observations on the impact of these emerging trends on the field of counselor education and training.

In the book *Pathways to Change* (1993), Selekman suggested that counselors might improve effectiveness by not adopting the position of privileged expert and instead consult with clients to help them rewrite previously unsatisfactory stories. From Selekman's perspective, counseling is seen as a collaborative and therapeutically flexible process, one in which a counselor focuses on client strengths, resources, key client words, and belief system material, as well as nonverbal behaviors (de Shazer, 1985; Gordon & Meyers Anderson, 1981; Selekman, 1993). Improvisation becomes a key ingredient of the counselor's clinical repertoire. Some examples of improvisation include "change talk" (Gingerich, de Shazer, & Weiner-Davis, 1988); surprise, playfulness, and humor; the use of a "miracle question" (de Shazer, 1988); "externalization of the problem" (White & Epston; 1990), "unique account" and "unique redescription" questions (White, 1988); and conversational questions (Anderson & Goolishian, 1988). By functioning as second order change agents, counselors give themselves permission to be more flexible and creative and increase the likelihood of meaningful change with clients.

According to Hoffman (1985), counselors using the second order change paradigm take on certain characteristics including the following: (a) an "observer" stance, (b) a collaborative structure, (c) an emphasis on the context for change, (d) lessened instrumentality, (e) circular assessment, and (f) a nonjudgmental view (p. 393). The following case example illustrates how one counselor used an observer stance, a collaborative structure, and a nonjudgmental view in helping a single mother resolve boundary issues with her teenage daughter.

Lynne was referred to the guidance center because of truancy problems at school, drug use, depression, suicidal ideation, and difficulties with authorities. She lived with her mother, who was attending a local university, although she also had had difficulties with depression and drugs. Early in the session, Lynne announced that she was pregnant. Adopting an observer position, the counselor began using key client words and belief material to join with the mother and daughter in order to help them begin to rewrite their problem-saturated story.

Client: After I have the baby I plan to go to Miami with my boyfriend. He has relatives there who will help us find a place to live.

Counselor: Sounds like you have an idea in mind for what you want to do. What do you think you would need to do today so things would work out the way you would like?

Client: I guess I'm going to have to start taking better care of myself physically.

Counselor: If you were to show me a videotape of how things will look over the next week as you begin to take better care of yourself, how would that look?

Rather than approaching the information as another problem pregnancy, the counselor continued to talk with the mother and daughter in a nonjudgmental manner attempting to create a collaborative structure that would provide mother and daughter with a context for change or at least for conversation.

Client: I'm really scared right now. We stand alone [meaning mother and daughter].

Counselor: I understand that being pregnant can be a frightening experience, especially if you are a teenager and there are few supports. Who else in your family is concerned about your being pregnant?

Client: Mom.

Counselor: When you have been scared, frightened, or overwhelmed in the past, how has your mom been helpful to you in working through these feelings?

Throughout the interview the counselor continued to use a more reflective style highlighted by positive connotations, a high tolerance for difference, and an avoidance of the idea of or term "acting-out" teenager. As a result of this approach the mother and adolescent felt understood and encouraged by a new level of awareness for each other's position.

The Counselor's Relationship With the Reflecting Team

While there is now an abundant literature available on the reflecting process (Andersen, 1987, 1991; Anderson & Goolishian, 1988; Anderson, Goolishian, & Winderman, 1986; Lax, 1989; Miller & Lax, 1988; Roberts, Caesar, Perryclear, & Phillips, 1989; Smith & Jenkins, 1991), we would like to focus on the relationship between the counselor and the reflecting team. Early observations of the reflecting process suggest that the approach (a) encourages therapeutic conversations between the counselor and clients (Hoffman, 1988); (b) expands the therapeutic decision-making process to include clients (Smith & Jenkins, 1991); and (c) provides a format for introducing sensitive topics that a counselor acting alone might avoid for fear of losing rapport with clients (Smith, Winton, & Yoshioka, 1992). In an attempt to research how clinicians experienced a reflecting process, Smith, Winton, and Yoshioka (1992) used a qualitative participant–observer methodology for interviewing counselors. Interestingly, they found that the use of a reflecting team was valuable when impasses were present and in providing multiple views for resolving a given problem. However, the authors did report that the process was not helpful if the reflections involved "aimless talk" or clients were not familiar with team practice.

The results of more recent research (Sells, Smith, Coe, Yoshioka, & Robbins, 1994; Smith, Sells, & Clevenger, 1994) seem to corroborate the earlier findings. The results of these studies again reinforce the idea of developing more ideas, perspectives, and frames as helpful in resolving therapeutic impasses. Clinicians reported that the process was not helpful when there were no major problems to solve or no crisis was present.

In the context of our work at the Akron Child Guidance Center, we focus on co-creating positive reframes during our discussions. As mentioned previously, the index clinician and team members briefly discuss any "stuck" areas before starting the session. We attempt to use presuppositional language such as "when" and "will," rather than "if," and "would," and the majority of time is spent on past, present, and future successes (Andersen, 1987). For example, a counselor might ask a client, "When your relationship with Mom (Dad, etc.) is going better, what will you be doing differently?" or "How will your relationship with Mom (Dad, etc.) be different when there is less stress between you?" The following case example illustrates our use of the reflecting team process with the family presented in the previous section.

The session centered on the daughter, Lynne, disclosing that she might be pregnant. After about 45 minutes the reflecting team entered the therapy room and mother, daughter, and counselor took positions behind the mirror. The following is a brief example of the reflecting team conversation:

Team Member 1: Once again, I see the bond of unconditional love being expressed between mother and daughter. What will happen to that bond if Lynne begins to take better care of herself physically and mother acts as a coach in the process?

Team Member 2: These women are becoming very competent. Mom has confidence in her daughter. Could it be that mother believes Lynne can handle other situations, like school, just like she is handling being pregnant?

Team Member 3: I wonder if having to face difficult situations doesn't bring forth the inner resources of mother and daughter?

Upon returning to the therapy room, daughter observes that "they got it right on the nose!"

Daughter: You know I felt kinda bummed out when I came here this morning, but now I feel much better. It feels good when you know someone else understands.

Mother: I guess I was wondering if I really was a good mom. Now I really believe I am.

In debriefing with the team following the session, the index counselor reported that the reflecting process provided support, lowered the family's anxiety, and provided numerous opportunities for reframes of the major problems. In a manner similar to observations of the counselors in the Sells et al. (1994) study, the counselor in this example emphasized how helpful it was to have the team draw out a specific theme (caring) because it helped decrease personal anxiety and created a context whereby both the counselor and family could get a different idea of the problem.

Impact of the Reflecting Team on Counselor Education

The following case example illustrates how the Akron Child Guidance reflecting team can be useful when a therapeutic system appears to be stuck.

Sam was a 44-year-old, divorced White male. Several years before becoming a client at Akron Child Guidance, Sam was briefly hospitalized in a psychiatric facility for depression, and at the time of his Child Guidance intake he was taking an antidepressant. A recovering alcoholic, he reported a long history of fighting while intoxicated, although at the time of the intake he was attending Alcoholics Anonymous meetings and had not fought since sobriety.

The client was the father of four children. His ex-wife died in an automobile accident about one year prior to his entering Akron Child Guidance. The client had a girlfriend, Linda, who was a recovering alcoholic and a victim of childhood incest. Formerly a heavy equipment operator, Sam was now on social security disability as a result of back and neck problems. His goals for therapy included a desire to be happier and more enthusiastic and to improve his relationships with his grown children and girlfriend.

In the presession discussion, the counselor offered that he felt stuck in the therapeutic process. Initially, the counselor was perceiving Sam's "story" as Sam's "problem." He reported that the previous sessions were filled with "gloom and doom" and he was wondering if it was time to move away from a solution-focused approach. The team members in their reflections encouraged him to look more at the relationship he was experiencing with the client and suggested the idea of a "see-saw" where he would exhibit a level of energy in the session to counterbalance Sam's pessimism and self-defeating words and thoughts. This suggestion gave the counselor a different way of joining with Sam and provided both Sam and the counselor an opportunity to view the environment through a different lens.

During the session, the counselor maintained a high energy level, used a variety of physical expressions to illustrate therapeutic issues, and introduced the metaphor of the client in a dinghy in the ocean, not knowing in which direction to paddle to reach land but knowing that a higher being was watching him and that he had strong hands with which to paddle. Then, knowing that Sam would have difficulty believing and accepting positive comments, the team decided to do a sculpt in which one team member took the role of a person on a dinghy at sea and the other two members represented distant shorelines. During the brief dialogue, the team's comments focused on the senses of seeing, feeling, and touching as ways of interacting with the environment in order to "find one's way." For example, despite being alone on the sea, the person could "see" the shoreline, "feel" hope, and use a hand (touch) to paddle the dinghy in a new direction.

The counselor described the client as "visibly moved" as he watched the drama unfold. During the switch, the client reported that before the session he felt lost and abandoned but the team had provided him with other ways of seeing things and the possibility of having a more satisfying life.

During the postsession, the counselor expressed the feeling that he had been given "permission" by the team to do things differently, and seeing the team likewise do things differently provided him with a new sense of confidence in his ability to work with Sam. While this "process" version of a reflecting position might at first glance seem different from previous examples, we believe the example is consistent with Andersen's conceptual formulation behind the reflecting position. Initially, the team selected a phrase previously used by the client ("a dinghy at sea") and then proceeded to provide an unusual extension of this metaphor to promote movement in the standstill system. In the sense that "one cannot not make a picture of the world" the team moved to visual and auditory reflections thereby allowing the counselor to become a participant-observer in the therapeutic system. We feel this example is a good illustration of an egalitarian approach to counseling and supervision.

Finally, as mentioned previously, the 1980s and 1990s provided counselors with innovative approaches for working with clients. We believe the coming decade will bring forth many new ideas and approaches for preparing counselors. For example, the social constructionist movement will challenge counselor educators to rethink and reorganize courses on theories and techniques. If counselor educators adopt the view that counseling is an egalitarian process involving a counselor as a participant-observer, then training programs based on the counselor as an expert in a hierarchical position will require restructuring. As counselor educators grapple with these ideas, previous ways for preparing counselors will give way to programs based on egalitarianism and relativism. We are excited by these possibilities for change and growth.

The Client and the Reflecting Position

Families that are seen by the reflecting team at Akron Child Guidance are usually stuck; that is, the stories they tell themselves and their counselors are different versions of past repetitive stories, with little possibility for different endings. The family's past has determined their present, and their past has become their present and future. Many of these families have lost the ability to rewrite their own stories. Their narratives of powerlessness and helplessness keep them stuck with unworkable solutions and old endings.

New endings, workable alternatives, and empowerment for these families can evolve through the process of co-creating therapeutic conversations with a reflecting team. These therapeutic conversations are created when the family and the reflecting team co-develop different meanings and different stories for the family's "stuckness."

How this process actually works for the family has more speculation than solid evidence (Smith, Yoshioka, & Winton, 1993), but it is assumed that the use of a reflecting team allows for the acceptance of numerous perspectives whereby the combination of the family members' perspectives create a "family reality" (Young et al., 1989). Family members can now look at themselves in new, safe, and nonthreatening ways. This new or different way of hearing and seeing themselves and others talk about their family story becomes a new reality, which is observer participant defined and co-constructed by the family and the reflecting team.

To lay the foundation for this new therapeutic reality, the first 30–40 minutes of therapy have focused on shifting family members' perspectives from being overly responsive to their own voices or having no voices to amplifying or giving voice to other family members' perspectives. Using conversation as the medium, the counselor looks for stories that are not being told or heard. Reflexive questions (Mishler, 1986; Tomm, 1988) are asked that allow for the loosening of meanings attached to the old family stories. Examples of reflexive questions include the following: "If as a new member of this family you wanted to convince your stepson that you really cared for him, how would you go about it?" "If your wife wanted her son to see more of your positive contributions to the family, what might she do?" (Tomm, 1988).

The family story about the problem, which had been laden with ambiguity, dualities, and rights and wrongs, becomes loosened as the conversation evolves. In this way, the co-created conversation of the counselor and family becomes the author of new possibilities. The therapeutic conversation becomes attached to the old story about the problem and creates an opening for change. As Andersen (1991) indicated, therapy becomes the continuous generation of meaning rather than the discovery of information. Therapy becomes conversation focused rather than hypothesis focused. The stage is now set for the reflecting team and the family to exchange positions. The observed become the observers, and the observers become the observed. While the reflecting team is sharing their thoughts on the counselor and family's conversation, the family is behind the mirror. Families have described this part of the process as "riveting" and "finally feeling understood." They stand at the mirror intent and focused on the reflecting team. Usually very little conversation is exchanged by family members during this period. They shift quickly from their roles of talkers to listeners, from active-participants to observer-participants. This metaposition the family has been placed in, coupled with the nonjudgmental and positively connoted conversation of the reflecting team, seems to free the family to hear and experience different ideas and multiple meanings about their problem story. Family members have said they see themselves in a new light: "Maybe our situation is not so bad. After all, the reflecting team doesn't think our family is so hopeless."

Often families have viewed their problems as being either/or, and the reflecting team has moved their understanding of their problem as being able to fit into a both/and story line. The multiple perspectives and musings of the reflecting team have provided the family with choices or alternatives. Alternatives, if heard and accepted, provide the family with the first openings between their either/or dichotomies. The idea of alternatives provides the family with a possible sense of control and power over the problem. These appropriate differences seem to be very helpful in moving the family to rewrite their problem story. When families have grasped the possibility of alternatives to their "stuckness," they often respond emotionally with tears of relief or become quietly contemplative.

At the end of the reflecting team conversation a second switch occurs with the family and the counselor moving back to the therapy room. The counselor will encourage family members to share their ideas and observations about the reflecting team's comments or the reflecting process. This last portion of the therapy will last from 5 to 20 minutes, depending on the family's needs or desires to share their thoughts. The following are some of the comments that family members have shared at this time:

—I liked hearing all of the ideas.
—We didn't know we had other choices.
—They seemed to know us so well.
—I liked the way they talked about our strengths.
—There were so many ideas, I didn't know what to comment on.
—It felt good to think our family has some control over what happens.
—Before I went behind the mirror I felt like they were spying on us; now I feel differently.

At this point, observers of the family will often comment on the family's different appearances. Family members appear more physically relaxed; their body language is more open. The climate in the room seems changed. Affect is lower, not as intense. Voices are quiet, less animated. Family members may change their seating arrangements, or move their chairs closer together. When asked to comment on these changes, family members will often respond that they feel "quieter," "calmer," and "more understood."

Concluding Statements

Reflecting teams provide an experiencing component for the family, followed by reflection on that experience. Families are offered experiential learning with built-in mechanisms for present-focused feedback (Yalom, 1983).

The reflecting team stance offers multiple and different views and voices that can free families to listen to their own "other" voices and views. When the family moves into the observation room to observe the reflecting team, it provides the family with a unique and novel way to gain a metaperspective. Becoming observers of the process, rather than being in the process, is a subtle way to teach the family how to experience and observe their own family processes.

The evolving and diminishing hierarchy between the family, the counselor, and the team offers the family a less rigid picture of roles. The move to a nonhierarchical stance sends the message to the family that they are important and valued in telling and creating new meanings and new family stories. A nonhierarchical stance also tends to demystify therapy. Rather than families becoming dependent on the counselor as the director or the expert, this position validates the families' own expert knowledge of their family and their problem.

Families report that the reflecting team process allows them to feel validated and more in control, because they are not only given feedback but also give feedback. This greater involvement in the therapy process can lead to a greater investment in the therapy outcome.

Family members also comment that hearing the team's observations couched in positive terms allows them to be more receptive to the team's different comments. Listening to the team's multiple views, offered in respectful and tentative ways, also provides another benefit for family members. Family members often pick up on the uncertainties of the team's conversation and comment that the team's uncertainty gives them permission to acknowledge uncertainty as okay and normal.

Overall, the view of families and counselors appears to suggest many benefits associated with a reflective team approach. The most often reported negative family evaluations of the reflecting team process focus on the lack of definitive answers provided by the team. Some families are left wondering what to do next. Conversational therapy may fit some families and some cultural groups better than others. In a very general sense, the reflecting team is part of the therapy culture, which is itself a reflection of the majority culture in America (Holiman & Lauver, 1987). The majority culture and perhaps in some instances the therapy culture may assume a "myth of sameness" for minority cultures, which may fail to account for a family's belief system and cultural and ethnic identity. Atkinson, Morton, and Sue (1993) emphasize the need for counselors to be cross-culturally competent and to have in their repertoire both verbal and nonverbal helping responses.

Reflecting teams tend to focus on the verbal, the story the family has been telling itself. However some families are nonconversational as a result of their personal style of relating, language barriers, gender roles, or family secrets such as physical or sexual abuse. These families may not as easily adapt or profit from conversational therapy. The reflecting team modality moves away from behavioral or nonverbal interventions that may more closely match a family's typical or more comfortable way of communicating. An editor of the present book suggested that we might have discovered an alternative solution in the form of "reflexive sculpting." We found this to be a very helpful observation, and one author of this chapter (Zarski) has started to use the idea in advanced practicum classes.

Another comment shared by family members is that there are often so many ideas being offered that there is little time to think about, comment on, or ask questions about their observations. Individuals report that it is often overwhelming to have several issues commented on during the same time period. Once again, the necessity of reading and meeting the family's need becomes of utmost importance. As a result of our work with reflecting teams, we continue to emphasize the autonomy of the family in determining the outcome.

For this reason it is always important to allow the family some time at the end of the session to give their own feedback or reflections, as well as ask any further questions about the process. In the case of a family that seems overwhelmed by the many ideas offered, the counselor might want to help them focus on one comment or idea that stood out as being important and take that one piece of information and reflect on that thought until the next session. Another intervention that can be useful with nonconversational or more concrete types of families is for the counselor to write down one thought from each member that they had about the reflecting team's comments. The counselor then gives the family members their written thoughts to take with them to be reflected on, and perhaps added to, until the next meeting.

For families that are also involved with other social service agencies, using a reflecting team format as the sole therapeutic modality may create tension for the family. Information can make a difference. When a family is involved with other service agencies it is often a good idea if the counselor schedules some time to educate the agency representatives about the purpose and process involved in using a reflecting team, possibly inviting them to observe a team. Taking a one-down position and asking permission to try something "appropriately unusual" with a family that has previously been stuck, may be all that is needed to give the counselor and the family freedom to work in a new way.

Many agency-referred families have lost the power to tell their own stories. Their narrative of helplessness and powerlessness has been coauthored by social service agencies. These families will often present with hidden narratives about the meanings of their stories. In these cases, if the reflecting team is not particularly sensitive to past, present, and future beliefs about the family's problem, and if they do not converse and ask questions concerning the meanings attached to these stories, therapy will stall and the stories will never have alternative endings.

In other words, the family members might be saying to themselves or each other different stories than they feel free or safe to tell other systems. The definition of *problems* is often shaped by larger system mandates. A family might story their adolescents' running away as "typical teenage behavior," while a social service agency might label the same behavior as "high risk" and in need of immediate attention.

There remain a number of questions for further consideration. For example, one might ask, "How does the reflecting process work?" "In what ways can a reflecting team remain in an appropriately unusual position?" "What is helpful in bringing a team member to a reflective position?"

So, as the preceding paragraphs have suggested, there are both potential positives and potential negatives to be considered when undertaking a reflective position, but we maintain that reflective conversations can be, and are, important ways to open up spaces for previously unthought of alternatives. It seems, then, that this process can be appropriately unusual for clients and may help them loosen their past meanings and stories about problems.

References

Andersen, T. (1987). The reflecting team: Dialogue and meta-dialogue in clinical and work. *Family Process*, *26*, 415–428.

Andersen, T. (Ed.). (1991). *The reflecting team: Dialogues and dialogues about the dialogues*. New York: Norton.

Anderson, H., & Goolishian, H. (1988). Human systems as linguistic systems: Evolving ideas about the implications for theory and practice. *Family Process*, *27*, 371–393.

Anderson, H., Goolishian, H., & Winderman, L. (1986). Problem-determined systems: Towards transformation in family therapy. *Journal of Strategic and Systemic Therapies*, *5*, 1–11.

Atkinson, D. R., Morton, G., & Sue, D. W. (1993). *Counseling American minorities: A cross-cultural perspective*. Dubuque, IA: W. C. Brown.

Bateson, G. (1951). Information and codification: A philosophical approach. In J. Ruesch & G. Bateson (Eds.), *Communication: The social matrix of psychiatry*. (pp. 168–211). New York: Norton.

Bateson, G. (1972). *Steps to an ecology of mind*. New York: Ballantine.

Bateson, G., Jackson, D. D., Haley, J., & Weakland, J. H. (1956). Toward a theory of schizophrenia. *Behavioral Science*, *1*, 251–264.

Boscolo, L., & Bertrando, P. (1993). *The times of time*. New York: Norton.

de Shazer, S. (1985). *Keys to solution in brief therapy*. New York: Norton.

de Shazer, S. (1988). *Clues: Investigating solutions in brief therapy*. New York: Norton.

de Shazer, S. (1994). *Words were originally magic*. New York: Norton.

Gergen, K. J. (1985). The social constructionist movement in modern psychology. *American Psychologist*, *40*, 266–275.

Gingerich, W., de Shazer, S., & Weiner-Davis, M. (1988). Constructing change: A research view of interviewing. In E. Lipchik (Ed.), *Interviewing* (pp. 21–31). Rockville, MD: Aspen.

Gordon, D., & Meyers-Anderson, M. (1981). *Phoenix: Therapeutic patterns of Milton H. Erickson.* Cupertino, CA: Meta.

Guttman, H. (1991). Systems theory, cybernetics, and epistemology. In A. S. Gurman & D. P. Kniskern (Eds.), *Handbook of family therapy* (Vol. 11, pp. 41–62). New York: Bruner/Mazel.

Hoffman, L. (1985). Beyond power and control: Toward a "second order" family systems therapy. *Family Systems Medicine, 3*, 381–396.

Hoffman, L. (1988). A constructivist position for family therapy. *Irish Journal of Psychology, 9*, 110–129.

Hoffman, L. (1991). A reflective stance for family therapy. *Journal of Strategic and Systemic Therapies, 10*, 4–17.

Holiman, M., & Lauver, P. J. (1987). The counselor culture and client-centered practice. *Counselor Education and Supervision, 26*(3), 184–191.

Lax, W. D. (1989). Systemic family therapy with young children in the family: Use of the reflecting team. *Psychotherapy and the Family, 5*, 55–73.

Maturana, H., & Varela, F. (1992). *The tree of knowledge.* Boston: Shambhala.

Miller, D., & Lax, W. (1988). Interrupting deadly struggles: A reflecting team model for working with couples. *Journal of Strategic and Systemic Therapies, 7*, 16–22.

Mishler, E. (1986). *Research interviewing: Context and narrative.* Cambridge, MA: Harvard University Press.

Roberts, M., Caesar, P. L., Perryclear, B., & Phillips. (1989). Reflecting team consultations. *Journal of Strategic and Systemic Studies, 8*, 38–46.

Selekman, M. D. (1993). *Pathways to change: Brief therapy solutions with difficult adolescents.* New York: Guilford Press.

Sells, S. F., Smith, T. E., Coe, M. J., Yoshioka, M., & Robbins, J. (1994). An ethnography of couple and therapist experiences in reflecting team practice. *Journal of Marital and Family Therapy, 20*, 247–266.

Smith, T., Winton, M., & Yoshioka, M. (1992). A qualitative understanding of reflective-teams II: Therapists' perspectives. *Contemporary Family Therapy, 14*, 419–432.

Smith, T., Yoshioka, M., & Winton, M. (1993). A qualitative understanding of reflecting teams I: Client perspectives. *Journal of Systemic Therapies, 12*(3), 28–43.

Smith, T. E., & Jenkins, D. (1991). *Reflecting teams: Voices of diversity.* Paper presented at the meeting of the Florida Association for Marriage and Family Therapy, Palm Beach Gardens, FL.

Smith, T. E., Sells, S., & Clevenger, T. (1994). Ethnographic content analysis of couple and therapist perceptions in a reflecting team setting. *Journal of Marital and Family Therapy, 20*, 267–286.

Tomm, K. (1988). Interventive interviewing: Part III. Intending to ask lineal, circular, strategic, and reflexive questions. *Family Process, 27*, 1–16.

von Glasersfeld, E. (1984). An introduction to radical constructivism. In P. Watzlawick (Ed.), *The invented reality.* New York: Norton.

Walter, J., & Peller, J. (1992). *Becoming solution-focused in brief therapy.* New York: Brunner/Mazel.

Whitaker, C. (1975). Psychotherapy of the absurd: With a special emphasis on the psychotherapy of aggression. *Family Process, 14*, 1–16.

White, M. (1988, Winter). The process of questioning: A therapy of literary merit? *Dulwich Centre Newsletter*, pp. 8–14. (Reprinted from *Selected Papers*, by M. White, 1989, Adelaide, Australia: Dulwich Centre Publications).

White, M., & Epston, D. (1990). *Narrative means to therapeutic ends.* New York: Norton.

Yalom, I. (1983). *Inpatient group psychotherapy.* New York: Basic Books.

Young, J., Perlesz, A., Paterson, R., O'Hanlon, B., Newbold, A., Chaplin, R., & Bridge, S. (1989). The reflecting team process in training. *Australian and New Zealand Journal of Family Therapy, 10(2)*, 69–74.

■ ■ ■

5

Family Counseling as Problem Dis-Solving and Collateral Learning: The Pragmatism of Harry Goolishian and G. Bob Gowin

Lyle J. White, PhD
M. Harry Daniels, PhD

Change is the raison d'être of counseling. People enter into a counseling relationship because something in their life is disturbing, and they want to change it. Despite the centrality of change to the counseling process, we, as pratictioners and educators, remain puzzled by the complexities of the concept. For example, how is change defined and determined in the context of family counseling? Whose voice (or voices) determine (a) which direction will change take? (b) how will change be assessed? and (c) will change be considered dynamic or static? These questions are not new ones; however, their relative urgency increases as the wishes and desires of more than one individual have to be conjointly considered, as in family counseling.

Until recently, definitions of change in modern Western societies have been structured by the notions of Cartesian dualism, the Newtonian worldview, and an unyielding conviction that truth is most apt to be found through the exclusive use of the scientific method. Recently, however, some social and behavioral scientists, therapists, and theoreticians have begun to question the pragmatics of structuring a worldview that emphasizes certainty and predictability as a means for constructing change, because the landscape of life appears more uncertain and complex. These thinkers have argued that meaning is a product of social discourse, that is, meaning is a social construction (Anderson & Goolishian, 1988; Epstein & Loos, 1989; Gergen, 1985). From a social constructionist perspective, the concept of change is not predetermined or fixed. Rather, its definition is arrived at through the shared discussions of those invested in a particular phenomena.

One of the leading voices in this discourse was Harry Goolishian. Although Goolishian is deceased, his colleagues (see Anderson, Goolishian, Pulliam, & Winderman, 1986; Epstein & Loos, 1989) at the Houston-Galveston Family Institute continue to search for practical ways of applying the notions of social constructionism to the practice of family counseling. In this chapter, we provide a brief review of Goolishian's innovative notions about the linguistic nature of change as it relates to the *dis-solution* of family problems and endeavor to make these ideas more accessible to practitioners by synthesizing Goolishian's notions with those presented by the educational philosopher D. Bob Gowin. We use a case study to illustrate the utility of this synthesis. Finally, we explain how this synthesis provides a set of suitable answers to the questions posed above.

Introduction to Goolishian's Linguistic Systems

Harry Goolishian and his associates at the Houston-Galveston Family Institute have contributed as much, if not more, than any other group of clinicians toward the application of the philosophy of social constructionism to the day-to-day work of family counselors (Hoffman, 1990, 1992; Markowitz, 1992). A comprehensive review of the work of this group of clinicians-theoreticians is, of course, beyond our means to present here. Their work has already filled numerous professional journals and chapters in edited books (cf. Anderson & Goolishian, 1985, 1988, 1990, 1992; Anderson, Goolishian, Pulliam, & Winderman, 1986; Anderson, Goolishian, & Winderman, 1986; Epstein & Loos, 1989; Goolishian, 1991; Goolishian & Anderson, 1987, 1990, 1992; Loos, 1991; Loos & Epstein, 1989; White, Summerlin, Loos, & Epstein, 1992), and we refer the interested reader to these original sources. Here our purpose is to encapsulate the basic tenants of Goolishian's work and to prepare the way for the synthesizing sections that follow.

Defining the Relevant System

Merleau-Ponty (1945/1962) observed some 50 years ago that humans are condemned to generate meaning about their observations and experiences. In tracing the philosophical roots of modern psychology and therapeutic practices, Goolishian (1988) noted that the *idea of a mind* is, among social constructionists, neither exogenic (i.e., the external world has priority in generating human knowledge) nor endogenic (i.e., the processes of the mind are preeminent). Rather the mind is intersubjective, a process that occurs *between* people. Social cultural systems are thus the product of social communication, not vice versa (Anderson & Goolishian, 1988). Meaning and understanding are socially and intersubjectively constructed, that is, it is through conversation that two or more people can come to an agreement that they are experiencing the same event in the same way (Anderson & Goolishian, 1988). Given this philosophical foundation, one of the fundamental goals of a social constructionist approach to counseling becomes that of trying to understand who is a part of this system of people who are generating meaning about a social problem. The relevant system can not be defined specifically a priori (i.e., the members of a family unit or a social institution); rather, it is defined linguistically. The definition of the relevant system evolves out of the social interactions that people have around a particular issue. Consequently, Goolishian and his colleagues initially labeled this a "problem-determined system" (Anderson, Goolishian, & Winderman, 1986). Later they changed their label to a "language-systems approach" (Anderson & Goolishian, 1988) in order to avoid the connotation that the membership of a system becomes fixed along with the problem definition.

During the course of counseling, knowledge is shared whether it is the history of a problem as seen by the client or the prognosis of a pathology as determined by the counselor's clinical experience or as indicated by accumulated research. According to the social constructionists' perspective (Gergen, 1982; Wittgenstein, 1963), knowledge systems are fundamentally linguistic systems. Knowledge becomes that which those involved in the linguistic system can agree on. Because counselors are engaged in discussing client problems and sharing knowledge, they also become part of the relevant linguistic system (cf., von Foerster, 1981; von Glasersfeld, 1986). Other individuals who do or do not attend counseling sessions may be a part of the relevant system as well. From the social constructionists' perspective, all those contributing to the evolving discussion around a problematic issue are members of the knowledge-linguistic system.

Defining the Counselor's Role

Because this knowledge-linguistic system occurs in the ongoing conversations that take place around a problem, the counselor's task is to find out who has participated in the meaning construction in the past, in the present, and is likely to participate in the future. The knowledge-linguistic systems are fluid and evolve continuously. Thus counselors, using this approach, will find themselves investigating the composition of the relevant system by asking questions such as "Who has been/is/should be talking with whom, about what, and in what way?"

The counselor's role is not to solve the presenting problem but to become a member of the knowledge-linguistic system as a participant-observer and as participant-manager of the conversations being conducted around the problem (Goolishian & Anderson, 1988). Family members are the experts in the content of the concern; the counselor is the expert in the conversational process around this concern (Goolishian & Anderson, 1990, 1992). As a conversation manager, the counselor's role is to keep the conversations about the problem ongoing. This can be accomplished by finding out who needs to be understood and by whom, and by creating an atmosphere in which perspectives can be broadened and new meanings constructed. Once new meanings about a presenting problem are constructed, then new possibilities for thinking about and acting on a problem can be created. For Goolishian, reconstruction of the problem provides the prospect for change.

In order to participate in and manage conversations so that problem reconstruction could occur, Goolishian suggested that counselors assume a "not knowing" posture with regard to the knowledge-linguistic system (Anderson & Goolishian, 1992). Other social constructionists have developed their own labels for this process. Cecchin (1987) likened it to an "invitation to curiosity" and taking a position of respect toward clients' efforts to solve their problems. Andersen (1992) has used the term "co-presence" to describe the counselor's role.

By taking a position of not knowing regarding the presenting problem and the knowledge-linguistic system, counselors do not abdicate the responsibility of accumulating knowledge about the issues that families present. Indeed, the not knowing position recognizes the uniqueness of families and the importance of coming to know that uniqueness. Elements of this not knowing perspective are present in the work of many therapists, even those outside the social constructionist arena. As noted by Minuchin and Nichols (1993), "therapists must be alert to their ignorance and willing to allow families to educate them" (p. 102). A not knowing position requires counselors to be curious about family issues as they are described in the professional literature, but more importantly as they are experienced by the members of the family. Information of this latter kind is best acquired through a process of exploration (i.e., conversation) rather than through the pretense of understanding.

The liability of traditional training is that through the emphasis given to the recognition of patterns and the reduction of symptoms into a specific problem definition, counselors will "arrive only at our own descriptions and explanations of the problem" (Goolishian & Anderson, 1988, p. 16). In contrast, a language systems approach to counseling acknowledges that there are so many possible permutations to the difficulties of living that one can never know with certainty all the important perceptions and "facts" related to each problem. In fact, given the fluid nature of social problems, it is likely that most knowledge is only temporary at best. The role of the counselor is to promote the continuation of these meaning-generating conversations until a problem can be constructed that is conceived by those in the relevant system as workable.

Defining and Developing a Workable Problem

In 1938, the philosopher Hans Lipps (cited in Anderson & Goolishian, 1988; Goolishian & Anderson, 1988) stated that any linguistic account carries with it a "circle of the unexpressed." More recently, Gadamer (cited in Anderson & Goolishian, 1988; Goolishian & Anderson, 1988) provided a similar observation and called it an "infinity of the unsaid," that is, that no matter how complete, clear, and univocal a communicative account may appear, new interpretations and meanings can be generated. Given these characteristics of a knowledge-linguistic system, problem definitions must be perceived as those that are developed, not discovered. Weick (1984) noted that "People often define social problems in ways that overwhelm their ability to do anything about it" (p. 40), that is, in ways that are unworkable and disallow change. Following this line of thinking, a counselor, reasoning as a social constructionist, has the task of helping people develop problem definitions that expand previous constructions, include the unsaid, and are workable.

To help the members of the relevant system look anew on a problem that has previously been defined in unworkable language and to help them reconsider the possibility of change, counselors need to begin by helping those individuals develop a narrative that states the problem in very specific, clear terms that they can agree on (similar to behavioral consultation approaches, cf. Bergan, 1977; Bergan & Tombari, 1976) . One part of that process (perhaps one of the first steps) is to find out what has not worked—so as to not find oneself in the position of recommending a previously unsuccessful course of action. Toward that end, counselors should ask questions such as, "What other solutions have been attempted?" "In what ways have they been helpful and not helpful?" "Under which circumstances has the problem been worse?" "Better?" "If there were to be some small changes that would suggest things were moving in the right direction, what would that look like?" "What has been the worst part about this problem?" "If there were no change in the problem, how long could it be tolerated?" "What would help to make things more tolerable, not necessarily 'better'"? "What ideas do other people have about this issue?"

In summary, developing a workable problem and the prospect of change is a collaborative undertaking in which the counselor reconstructs the dilemma with family members and others within the relevant knowledge-linguistic system. The problem definition that emerges will, of course, depend on the system members' previous experiences and constructions and on the counselor's ability to manage conversation, that is, the language used to compose questions and cultivate dialogue (Loos, 1991). The counselor's task is to help create a descriptive narrative about the problem that is meaningful (i.e., relevant to the participants' concerns), that is coherent (i.e., makes sense to the family and other members of the relevant system), and that provides new options for effective action in the situation confronting them (i.e., the client's feel they can now do something to positively affect the dilemma).

Case Illustration

One of Harry Goolishian's favorite stories (personal communication, December, 1988) about the beginnings of family counseling was that he and other pioneers had to violate the professional conventions of the time in order to provide clinical services to both members of a couple, either separately or conjointly. However, in doing so, he discovered that the descriptions that one partner would have of the marital relationship differed significantly from the descriptions provided by the other. On many occasions, the descriptions would be so disparate that he found it difficult to imagine that the partners were talking about the same set of events or even the same relationship. Through experiencing these differing views, Goolishian came to recognize that the manner in which problems are defined is always determined by the parties involved in the discussion about the problem rather than by a reality intrinsic to the problem.

The following example illustrates the wisdom and utility of Goolishian's observations about how the hope for change (as a view of family members) creates the prospect for change. It also illustrates how change can occur within a knowledge-linguistic system.

This case involved a family of four,—mother, father, a 16-year-old boy, and a 14-year-old girl—who consulted with the first author about the boy's academic performance. The presenting problem centered around the boy's inability to perform academically in a manner that was consistent with his parents' expectation and the parents' inability to reconcile their differences about the reasons for the boy's poor performance. The family saw themselves as conventional in both social and professional realms, and indeed, the issues they presented were not atypical for families with school age children experiencing learning difficulties. The family seemed to want a simple and quick solution to an ill-defined and persistent problem. Yet, they insisted on respect from the consultant and their own active involvement in defining their problem. The issues of respect and involvement were especially important to the members of this family because they had not been in counseling before and were put off by the notion that they had to seek outside help for a family problem. With this family, it was absolutely necessary for the consultant to demonstrate respect for all family members so that each would accept him as a member of the knowledge-linguistic system.

Interestingly, during the process of negotiating a consulting contract, the differences in the parents' attributions about the causes of the boy's problems became obvious to the consultant. The focus of the difference was not whether the boy was experiencing difficulty at school; rather, it was how to interpret or explain these difficulties and how to decide what was the appropriate course of action to take in order to remedy the situation. From the consultant's perspective, this family was experiencing a dilemma that they were ill-equipped to resolve without first possessing new facts and some new conceptual structures. On one hand, the members of the family saw themselves as a cohesive unit with clearly defined external boundaries. On the other hand, each claimed their individual explanation and their right to hold it. In dealing with this particular dilemma, the family members were acting out for the consultant their reasons for seeking consultation. From a social constructionist perspective, it was evident that the family needed to extend the boundaries of its relevant system in order to generate new information. Thus the consultant was invited to become a member of the knowledge-linguistic system.

The family situation was further complicated by the fact that the 16-year-old son had just received his driver's license and a gift of a pick-up truck from his paternal grandfather, and he was learning to enjoy the gift and the freedom it provided. In addition, he had recently begun to receive peer recognition for his athletic endeavors, and this encouraged him to devote his energies toward athletics instead of academics. From his perspective, the poor school performance was related only to the lack of attention he gave to it. Not surprisingly, then, he did not see himself as the justified focus of family attention. In fact, he took exception to his parents' suggestion that he was the source of his family's worry or that his behavior needed changing.

From the consultant's perspective, the experience of being with this family was initially puzzling. The consultant was uncertain if a psychoeducational evaluation would allow the family to coalesce around a problem that they could work together to resolve, or if the evaluation would serve to accentuate the differences in opinion that already existed. As the consultant listened to family members explain their perspectives, it became clear that family members listened to one another, but they had not discovered ways to accommodate each other's perspectives. In social constructionist terms, the family had been unable to co-construct a workable problem.

In addition to providing the family with new, psychoeducational evaluation information about the boy's academic difficulties, the consultant hoped to involve the family in developing together an interpretation based on this new information. By developing a mutually agreeable interpretation, family members increased the probability that they could work together toward the dis-solution of this problem. In doing so, the consultant helped the family find new meaning about the events that represented the boy's problem.

Before describing how the consultant helped the family develop a mutually agreeable interpretation that would lead to problem dissolution, we want to describe the process of change in family counseling from a social constructionist perspective. The ability to change is linked to the ability to find new meaning about events through conversations. In the following section we integrate the work of two social constructionists, Harry Goolishian and D. Bob Gowin, and illustrate how this integration was used in the aforementioned case study.

Change: Finding Meaning in Conversations About Events

Our clinical experience informs us that therapeutic conversations with families could be considered as either information-gathering or information-generating phenomena. This dilemma brings up the question "How do we organize and manage information so that it may be used to the client's benefit?" The information-gathering strategy is prescriptive, that is, information is gathered from the client (or key informants) and then compared with professionally determined behavioral descriptors, such as those in the *DSM-IV* (*Diagnostic and Statistical Manual of Mental Disorders*, 4th ed.; American Psychiatric Association, 1994). By substantiating a match between the gathered information and the criterion descriptors, the counselor makes an appropriate (hopefully) diagnosis. With the diagnosis in mind, treatment becomes a matter of applying the best of what is known about clinical practice to the identified problem. In this instance, the agreed on behavioral descriptors, diagnosis, and best clinical practice are the products of a particular theoretical worldview that allows certain value claims and advocates certain criteria for excellence or change and disallows and opposes others. Once the behavioral descriptors have been sufficiently defined and matched, the prescribed treatment is more or less determined. The problem and its treatment seem to exist independently of the meaning that the client, as well as others affiliated with the client and the problem, assigns to it.

When viewed as an information-generating process, the counseling interview takes on a different perspective. In choosing to forgo (at least temporarily) the use of predetermined professional schemes for gathering and organizing information, the counselor is in a better position to acknowledge and incorporate the client's meaning about events into a definition of the problem.

Consequently, the meaning of the problem and the subsequent therapeutic treatment are developed through the conversation between the client and counselor; it is not found in the behavioral criteria–treatment match as defined by a society of professionals. We are not advocating the complete abandonment of this traditional and familiar way of working with clients. Rather, we want to emphasize two things: (a) human behavior is complex and (b) the meaning of human behavior is generated through conversation.

If counselors focus too intently on codified criteria (e.g., *DSM-IV*, *International Classification of Diseases-9*, World Health Organization guidelines; cf. Quay & Werry, 1986), they may miss some of the important nuances imbedded within the complexity of the problem, that is, nuances that contribute significantly to the meaning assigned to the situation by their clients. The nuances are important to consider because in them, counselors and clients may discover the basis for developing a problem that can be resolved.

From this perspective, it is important to acknowledge that information about the problem, and its meaning, is generated through counselor–client conversations. Clients' problems are not uncovered by counselors through conversations; rather, they are developed through a sharing of the meaning of the events surrounding the problem.

Meaning and Educating

Gowin (1981) has asserted that the meaning an individual assigns to an event represents the integration of the individual's thinking, feeling, and acting about that event. Thus, when clients are talking about a problem, we assume that they are presenting their meaning system about an event or series of events. Gowin has defined an event in this way: When an occurrence is observed by three individuals, at least two will agree that it happened (p. 29). It is the occurrence of events that provides the basis of Gowin's "event epistemology." We contend that client problems begin as events, or occurences, and thus, understanding the meaning of these events to clients serves as the basis for the development of a problem-based "event epistemology."

For Gowin, an event epistemology has both conceptual and factual domains. He has used a "V" heuristic as a visual scheme to illustrate how individuals organize their understanding of an event or a series of events hierarchically into personal meaning systems (see Figure 1). The "V" illustrates the relationship between the conceptual and factual domains of events at different conceptual levels. Gowin has argued that the modern practice of education (and, consequently, counselor education) emphasizes the right-hand side of the "V," that is, the methodological and factual domain, and gives

FIGURE 1
Conceptual and factual domains of an event epistemology.

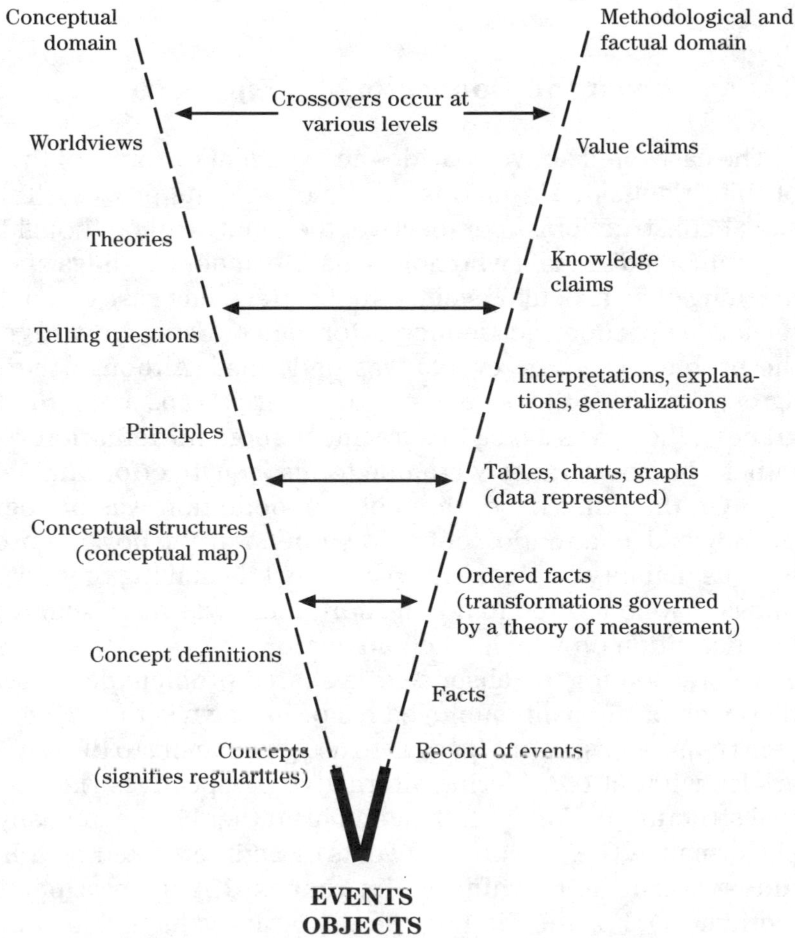

little attention to the conceptual domain. In this way, the value claims that one makes determine the criteria of excellence for signifying an event, the knowledge claims made about the event, and eventually how records of events are kept. In short, the methodological and factual domains determine the meanings ascribed to new events. Events not circumscribed by existing method or fact are either ignored or transformed in such a way that they fit within accepted knowledge claims. Thus, problems not circumscribed by codified diagnostic criteria may be ignored or transformed in such a way that they depart from (or ignore altogether) the meaning system of the client.

Change From the Counselor's Perspective

The case cited above provides an excellent example of the limits of this "right-sided" thinking on the counseling process. Taking a social constructionist perspective, the family can be thought of as a group of individuals who hold separate understandings about the meaning of a particular event,—in the preceding case example, the teenage son's poor academic performance. Using Gowin's model, the problem (i.e., the event) was undefined. Although there was agreement about the occurrence of the event (i.e., a record of poor grades), there was a lack of agreement about its definition. For the father, the poor grades were due to inadequate effort and motivation. On the other hand, the mother's definition was biological—the boy had an attention deficit disorder. For the boy, the problem was his inability to please his parents while making time to do the things that he wanted to do. In short, there was not a shared problem definition on which all could agree.

The reason for the absence of a shared problem definition was that each participant employed his or her own set of value claims (see right-hand side of Figure 1) to assign meaning to the boy's poor grades without considering alternative perspectives (i.e., conceptual structures). For the father, and his father before him, any poor performance (i.e., record of events) was interpreted as a lack of industriousness (a value claim that is driven by a particular worldview). For the mother, the important value claim was to be loving, nurturing, and nonjudgmental of her son. Consequently, her event definition was one in which concern rather than blame was expressed. By assigning a biological basis for the poor grades, she was able to express concern while continuing to be loving and nurturing. The boy did not want to adopt either of his parent's meanings and elected instead to explain the poor grades in terms of being expected by his parents to do too much and by his teachers' unwillingness or inability to provide adequate instruction.

In their effort to resolve (i.e., conjointly define) their problem, the family sought out the first author and asked for a psychoeducational evaluation of the boy. In so doing, the family demonstrated a willingness to suspend their knowledge claims about the behavior and invite an alternative explanation. In responding to the invitation, the author developed an alternative meaning system about the boy's problem by creating a series of new events, that is, a protocol of psychoeducational assessments. Taken together, the results of the assessment became a new record of events. These facts (i.e., record of events) were then ordered and represented in psychometric terms and then tentatively interpreted by the consultant using psychoeducational concepts and definitions.

When the consultant met with the family to discuss his observations, he introduced new and different facts, the results of the assessment. He also introduced alternative conceptual structures for organizing previously held facts. In doing so, he encouraged the family members to reevaluate their knowledge claims about the problem and to discuss their conceptual definitions. The evaluator's participation in the family's conversation emphasized both the right and left sides of the "V." In short, the family and the consultant shared their respective meaning systems about the event (problem), and because of conceptual dissimilarities that became apparent, the family's conversation about the boy's behavior was altered. Consequently, because of the altered conversation, a new meaning system—one that allowed for new ways of thinking, feeling, and acting—was generated.

Having discussed change and the case example from both Goolishian's and Gowin's theoretical perspective, we are now ready to procede with the integration of these two social constructions. First, we consider change from the counselor's perspective. Next, using the case example, we demonstrate the practical value of our integration.

Change From the Clients' Perspective

Client families enter counseling because they want to change some feature of their lives. In our view, Goolishian and Gowin are conceptually linked in that each has contended that change is more likely to occur when those who have a vested interest in problem resolution (i.e., part of the language system) are actively involved in its definition. Counselors contribute to this process of problem dis-solution in two ways. First, they lend their expertise by introducing new facts and concepts for the family to consider in their interpretations of and conceptualization about their problems. In the case example presented above, the counselor, because of his training as a school psychologist, was able to both hear the problem definitions presented by individual family members and add other plausible explanations, which served to expand the conversation about the problem. Second, and perhaps more important, counselors manage the conversation so that all involved may be heard (i.e., there is a sharing of meaning systems among members of the relevant system). Again, in the foregoing example, the counselor found a way to respect each family member's definition of the problem even though they were varied and, in some instances, contradictory. By doing so, the counselor enabled each family member to be heard, and in turn, to hear one another.

It is our experience that client families have mixed feelings and responses to counseling through a knowledge-linguistic system. On one hand, the absence of the structure of "counselor-as-expert" creates some emotional discomfort in that clients are not told how to solve their problems. In a positive sense, the conversational tone of the initial interview helps to minimize some of the anxieties associated with a clinical setting, that is concerns about being evaluated or judged to be at fault. Despite clients' initial sense of unfamiliarity and initial discomfort, most seem to adapt easily to this approach to counseling.

The generation of a collaborative approach to problem definition and dis-solution as well as the development of an event epistemology is a statement of respect that counselors can extend to clients. When the client accepts the respect as genuine, this statement promotes involvement, cooperation, collaboration, and ultimately, a sense of personal agency.

Conclusion

In this chapter we have attempted to define how change occurs within the context of family counseling by describing a knowledge-linguistic systems model that invites all those involved in the discussion about a problem to determine the direction that change is to take. Counseling from a knowledge-linguistic systems model assumes that change is dynamic and that determing the effectiveness of change at any point in time is reserved for those currently participating in the system.

Integrating Goolishian and Gowin

The knowledge-linguistic model that we have described is based on the work of two social constructionists, Harry Goolishian and D. Bob Gowin. Both have declared that it is through conversation between two or more people that the meaning of events is determined. Goolishian construed counseling systems as linguistic systems in which knowledge is shared and meaning is co-constructed around an event or problem by the clients and the counselor. Gowin has defined educating as the sharing of meaning systems, where a meaning system represents the integration of an individual's thinking, feeling, and acting about an event. Our integrated model emphasizes Goolishian's rich use of language and Gowin's visual heuristics. Both writers have argued that shared meaning is the core of social constructionism. Thus therapeutic conversations produce both an exchange of knowledge and collateral learning.

Thinking about counseling as an exchange of knowledge and collateral learning has implications for counselors and counselor educators alike. Two of the more significant implications are described below.

Counselors and Clients as Learners

Individuals are attracted to the counseling profession for a variety of reasons. One common reason is the desire to help others. To help another means different things to different people. Using the integrated model described previously may not be suitable to all counselors because doing so requires certain therapeutic skills, including a high tolerance for ambiguity, cognitive flexibility, and a worldview that embraces, rather than minimizes, the complexity of the human condition. In this counseling model, counselors as well as their clients share a collateral role of "learner."

When counselors view their clients and themselves as collateral learners within an educating environment, the focus of counseling is on the generation of new facts and the exploration of alternative conceptual structures that will help interpret, explain, and dis-solve the presenting problem. We believe that this position provides the counselor and the client greater flexibility to consider alternative ways of thinking about presenting problems. Perhaps the greatest advantage of this model is that it does not rely on diagnostic labels (e.g., victim of poor teaching, lazy, unmotivated, attention-disordered) previously used to describe the client's situation. The reliance on diagnostic labels often reifies labels, treating abstractions as fixed and certain knowledge about the meaning of behavior. In contrast, when the client and counselor see themselves as learners, the importance of diagnostic labels is reduced, and the importance of interpersonal involvement, cooperation, collaboration, and ultimately, personal agency is increased.

Training Counselors to Be Learners

The integrated model described in this chapter provides an alternative strategy for thinking about the counselor–client relationship and the conduct of counseling itself. The essential difference is that we do not see counseling as a process of fixing clients' problems. In fact, like Goolishian (Goolishian & Anderson, 1988) we question the utility of the assumption that problems can be fixed in any permanent way. Thus it may not be useful to endeavor to reduce uncertainty with a fixed diagnosis. The insistence on certainty and solving problems is linked to a mechanistic worldview that has permeated the social and behavioral sciences in general, and family counseling in particular (cf., Dell & Goolishian, 1981; Hoffman, 1992).

Once counselors can accept that they need not obligate themselves to fix the presenting problem, then they are free to accept the role of a collateral learner who is in conversation with the client and free to explore the "circle of the unexpressed" or the "infinity of the unsaid" as discussed by Lipps and Gadamer (cited in Goolishian & Anderson, 1988). Exploring the unexpressed and the unsaid requires interpersonal communication skills that are familiar to counselors and introduced in most counselor education programs. In addition to these foundational skills, circular questions (Fleuridas, Nelson, & Rosenthal, 1986; Palazzoli Selvini, Boscolo, Cecchin, & Prata, 1980; Penn, 1982), curiosity (Cecchin, 1987), reflection of co-presence (Andersen, 1992; Wangberg, 1991), and not knowing (Anderson & Goolishian, 1992) have, in our experience, enabled counselor trainees to engage clients in conversations about their presenting problems and construct alternatives that allow for their dis-solution.

In taking a position as a collateral learner, the counselor's theoretical worldview, value claims, and standards for determining excellence are temporarily suspended, and total attention is directed toward understanding the meaning of the event for the clients. When meaning is co-constructed through relational conversation, the communicators need only a desire to be co-present with the other and a willingness to remain involved in the conversation.

References

American Psychiatric Association. (1994). *Diagnostic and statistical manual of mental disorders* (4th ed). Washington, DC: Author.

Andersen, T. (1992). Reflections on reflecting with families. In S. McNamee & K. J. Gergen (Eds.), *Therapy as social construction* (pp. 54–68). Sage: London.

Anderson, H., & Goolishian, H. (1985). Systems consultation to agencies dealing with domestic violence. In L. Wynne, S. McDaniel, & T. Weber (Eds.), *The family therapist as consultant* (pp. 284–299). New York: Guilford.

Anderson, H., & Goolishian, H. (1988). Human systems as linguistic systems: Evolving ideas about the implications for theory and practice. *Family Process, 27*, 371–393.

Anderson, H., & Goolishian, H. A. (1990). Beyond cybernetics: Comments on Atkinson and Heath's "Further thoughts on second-order family therapy." *Family Process, 29*, 157–163.

Anderson, H., & Goolishian, H. (1992). The client as the expert: A not knowing approach to therapy. In S. McNamee & K. Gergen (Eds.), *Social-construction and therapeutic process* (pp. 25–39). Newbury Park, CA: Sage.

Anderson, H., Goolishian, H., Pulliam, G., & Winderman, L. (1986). The Galveston Family Institute: Some personal and historical perspectives. In D. Efron (Ed.), *Journeys: Expansions of the strategic and systemic therapies* (pp. 97–122). New York: Brunner/Mazel.

Anderson, H., Goolishian, H., & Winderman, L. (1986). Problem determined systems: Towards transformation in family therapy. *Journal of Strategic and Systemic Therapies*, 5, 1–14.

Bergan, J. R. (1977). *Behavioral consultation*. Columbus, OH: Charles E. Merrill.

Bergan, J. R., & Tombari, M. L. (1976). Consultation skill and efficiency at the implementation of outcomes of consultation. *Journal of School Psychology, 14*, 3–14.

Cecchin, G. (1987). Hypothesizing, circularity, and neutrality revisited: An invitation to curiosity. *Family Process, 26*, 405–413.

Dell, P. F., & Goolishian, H. A. (1981). "Order through fluctuation": An evolutionary epistemology for human systems. *Australian Journal of Family Therapy, 2*, 175–184.

Epstein, E. S., & Loos, V. E. (1989). Some irreverent thoughts on the limits of family therapy: Toward a language-based explanation of human systems. *Journal of Family Psychology, 2*, 405–421.

Fleuridas, C. L., Nelson, T. S., & Rosenthal, D. M. (1986). The evolution of circular questions: Training family therapists. *Journal of Marital and Family Therapy, 12*, 113–127.

Gergen, K. J. (1982). *Toward transformation in social knowledge*. New York: Springer-Verlag.

Gergen, K. J. (1985). The social constructionist movement in modern psychology. *American Psychologist, 40*, 266–275.

Goolishian chosen to receive AAMFT distinguished professional contribution to family therapy award. (1991, August). *AAMFT Family Therapy News*, AAMFT Annual Conference Supplement, p. 3.

Goolishian, H. A. (1988, May). The very idea of a mind. *Psychiatry in the year 2000—The challenge of synthesis*. Symposium conducted at the University of Texas Health Science Center Medical School, Department of Psychiatry and Behavioral Sciences, Houston, TX.

Goolishian, H., & Anderson, H. (1987). Language systems and therapy: An evolving idea. *Journal of Psychotherapy, 24*, 529–538.

Goolishian, H. A., & Anderson, H. A. (1988, July). *From family to systemic therapy and beyond*. Paper presented at the Second International Congress of the International Society for Adolescent Psychiatry, Geneva, Switzerland.

Goolishian, H., & Anderson, H. (1990). Understanding the therapeutic system: From individuals and families to systems in language. In F. Kaslow (Ed.), *Voices in family psychology* (pp. 91–113). Newbury Park, CA: Sage.

Goolishian, H., & Anderson, H. (1992). Strategy and intervention versus non-intervention: A matter of theory? *Journal of Marital and Family Therapy, 18*, 5–15.

Gowin, D. B. (1981). *Educating*. Ithaca, NY: Cornell University Press.

Hoffman, L. (1990). Constructing realities: An art of lenses. *Family Process, 29*, 1–12.

Hoffman, L. (1992). An appreciation of Harry. *Family Process, 31*, 101–102.

Loos, V. E. (1991). Construing couples: The challenges of marital therapy. *International Journal of Personal Construct Psychology, 4*, 293–312.

Loos, V. E., & Epstein, E. S. (1989). Conversational construction of meaning in family therapy: Some evolving thoughts on Kelly's sociality corollary. *International Journal of Personal Construct Psychology, 2*, 149–167.

Markowitz, L. M. (1992, January/February). Harold Goolishian, 1924–1991. *The Family Therapy Networker*, Vol. 16(1) 12–13.

Merleau-Ponty, M. (1962). *Phenomenology of perception* (C. Smith, Trans.). London: Routledge & Kegan Paul (Original work published 1945)

Minuchin, S., & Nichols, M. P. (1993). *Family healing: Tales of hope and renewal from family therapy*. New York: Free Press.

Palazzoli Selvini, M., Boscolo, L., Cecchin, G., & Prata, G. (1980). Hypothesizing-circularity-neutrality: Three guidelines for the conductor of the session. *Family Process, 19*, 3–12.

Penn, P. (1982). Circular questioning. *Family Process, 21*, 267–280.

Quay H. C., & Werry, J. S. (Eds.) (1986). *Psychopathologial disorders of childhood*. New York: Wiley.

von Foerster, H. (1981). *Observing systems*. Seaside, CA: Intersystems Publications.

von Glasersfeld, E. (1986). Steps in the construction of "others" and reality: A study in self-regulation. In R. Trappl (Ed.), *Power, autonomy, utopia: New directions toward complex systems*. New York: Plenum.

Wangberg, F. (1991). Self reflection: Turning the mirror inward. *Journal of Strategic and Systemic Therapies, 10(3)*, 18–29.

Weick, K. E. (1984). Small wins. *American Psychologist, 39*, 40–49.

White, L., Summerlin, M. L., Loos, V., & Epstein, E. (1992). School and family consultation: A language-systems approach. In M. Fine & C. Carlson (Eds.), *Handbook of family-school interventions: A systems perspective* (pp. 347–362). Boston: Allyn & Bacon.

Wittgenstein, L. (1963). *Philosophical investigations.* (G. Anscombe, Trans.). New York: MacMillian.

■ ■ ■

PART III

SOCIAL CONSTRUCTION THEORY AND COUNSELOR EDUCATION

6

Tom Andersen's Comments on Reflecting Processes and Some Observations on Reflecting Practices in Supervision

Jane A. Cox, PhD
Nadene A. L'Amoreaux, MA

Tom Andersen, a psychiatrist from Norway, is perhaps best known for his ideas on reflective thinking and is the originator of the related reflecting team process. Much of his writing has been about his experiences with and thoughts on the use of reflecting teams in family therapy (Andersen, 1987, 1989, 1991, 1992, 1995). He has also written about the potential for innumerable variations of the reflecting team process, one being its possible use in supervision (Andersen, 1995, p. 19). The authors were interested in Andersen's thoughts on reflection, reflecting teams, and counselor supervision, and he shared his ideas with them during an interview in April 1996.[1]

What follows in this chapter are some of Andersen's ideas about his work, which he shared during his interview with the authors.[2] During

[1] The word *supervision* was initiated by the authors, not by Andersen. Andersen said that he does not like to be called a supervisor, that he prefers to say that he works with people or talks with people.

[2] All quoted material was taken from this interview unless otherwise cited.

this interview, Andersen described premises that are important to his work, including ideas about (a) human beings, (b) language, and (c) change and development. From this starting point, Andersen discussed ideas about working with supervisees who are seeing families for counseling. As further background for Andersen's comments, this chapter begins with a brief description of the reflecting team process, as well as Andersen's description of how he became interested in this process. At the conclusion of this chapter is a description of the authors' experience with an adaptation of the reflecting team process for use in the supervision of counselors-in-training.

The Reflecting Team Process

As mentioned in the fourth chapter of this book, the reflecting team process has been used as a means of working with families who are in counseling. In such instances, before counseling proceeds, two teams are formed—an interview team and a reflecting team. The interview team consists of an interviewer (the family's counselor or perhaps another clinician) and the family coming for counseling. The reflecting team often consists of counseling professionals but may at times include family members. To begin the process, the interview team discusses the family's concerns while the reflecting team silently listens at a distance, perhaps in an adjoining room with a two-way mirror or simply in a separate section in the same room. Following the interview team's discussion, the reflecting team members speak to one another, sharing ideas that come to their minds, while the interview team silently listens. The discussion may then shift back to the interview team, as they reflect on the reflecting team's conversation. There could be one or two or several shifts between the interview team and the reflecting team. Andersen stressed that there could be many variations of this process and that it could be used in a variety of situations in addition to counseling settings (Andersen, 1991, 1995).

Andersen (1989) wrote that one of the benefits of the reflecting team process lies in the process itself; "the shift between being a talking participant and a listening participant around the same issues seems to be a very powerful process in order to create new descriptions and explanations" (p. 75). Other benefits included "1. an increasing feeling of equality and respect between team and the family; 2. instant feedback to the team; 3. potential for the co-evolution of understanding of the family's problems and possibilities for change between family, therapist and team" (p. 75).

When asked during our conversation how he became interested in the reflecting team process, Andersen recalled his experiences in the early 1980s. At that time, referring to his work in therapy, Andersen described how he was "uncomfortable being the person to tell people how to live their lives," saying that such an expert position had become increasingly uncomfortable for him. His meeting with members of the Milan group in 1981 provided some relief for his discomfort; the Milan group was using a method of therapy that Andersen described as more collaborative and less hierarchical. Yet Andersen said that he still wondered if his work could be "done differently." So, in 1985, Andersen and his colleagues began to share their thoughts with each other in the presence of their clients. With these "open talks as the reflecting team represents," Andersen found a way "to get out of the [expert] position"

When recounting this history of using reflecting teams, Andersen mentioned to us that their use existed in practice for some time before a description of the process was recorded or before a theoretical framework for reflecting teams was developed. This is consistent with how Andersen described his approach to research. In his view, speculation follows experience; "We go out into the world and experience things, just do the work and experience and then we go on and speculate, 'What was this? What was this all about?'" Regarding his speculation following some of his experiences with reflecting teams, Andersen commented that questions about the nature of human beings, language, and change and development began to appear.

Premises to Andersen's Comments About Supervision

During the interview, Andersen noted three premises that are important to his work: (a) his understanding of who human beings are, (b) his understanding of the use of language, and (c) his ideas about change and development. The remainder of this chapter will relate to these premises.

Nature of Human Beings

Regarding his understanding of human beings, Andersen described how he does not think of a person as a set of certain abilities or characteristics. Nor does he think of a person as the result of psychological, biological, or sociological structures. Rather, Andersen conceives of a person as "a very active being in the world in this moment." He views this as a similarity shared by all people (clients, supervisees, and others), that a person is living in "this moment," so that it is this moment that "counts." And it is in this moment that a person will choose the next step. For Andersen, life is "to be in the moment to choose between possibility steps." And the way that a person is present in the moment, preparing for the next step, is what moves the person into the person she or he becomes. Therefore, Andersen focuses his attention on the present moment, movement, and possible movements from which the (other) person may choose.

Nature of the Use of Language

Another of Andersen's assumptions about human beings is that they are always in motion, that people's bodies are constantly active and moving. This activity is found in both language and in physical movement. In a discussion of language, the second concept important to Andersen's work, Andersen described his understanding of language as an "activity" that consists of both the uttering of words and the movement of our bodies. This combination of uttering and moving can be thought of as a "repertoire," with each person having a repertoire for self-expression. With a supervisee, as with a client or any other person with whom he is working, Andersen searches to find where the person is in terms of self-expression. He is careful to not impose his language, metaphors, or thoughts on the other person. Rather, Andersen attempts to "be in the other person's language" and from her or his language converses with them about what future steps the person might take.

Andersen also discussed expression, through both language and body movement, as being informative and formative. Expressions are informative in that they convey to others what one thinks. They can also be thought of as formative because expressions of language and movement help people find meaning; meaning does not precede language and movement but rather follows from it. As one talks one "reaches toward the meaning." Therefore, if we speak differently, we find other meanings. In Andersen's words, "The meaning does not come first. The meaning comes in the end. That is another assumption about language....So if we speak differently, we reach another thought, we reach another meaning." And not only does language form the meaning, but Andersen also described how language forms a "whole person"; "talking formed the meaning, and actually the talking formed a whole person, formed a person to be sad or to be happy or to be angry or to be quick or to be lazy, so that is the formative part."

Nature of Change and Development

When discussing change and development, the third premise to understanding Andersen's comments about supervision, he described two types of change. One type of change is change that limits or constrains a person and the other type allows for expansion. Change that constrains is change that limits a person's existing repertoire of language and physical movement. One example of this that Andersen shared was that if a person can walk, run, and jump, a limiting change may constrain the person so that he or she can no longer jump, they can only walk and run. This type of change could be viewed as controlling, oppressing, forcing, or training people not to do certain things. Such change may come from within people, for example, if they tell themselves that they are bad people. But often such change originates from outside the person, as when a clinician tries to correct or limit a person's symptoms by constraining his or her repertoire.

The second type of change that Andersen described is change that does not limit, but rather change that brings out something new, change that encourages expansion and renewal in a person's existing repertoire of language and movement. Such change comes from within a person rather than from without and brings out something new by expanding on what is already there. Therefore, Andersen sees his contribution in supervision as being with the supervisee in such a way that the supervisee's "self" expands. But before expansion can take place, he first searches for where the person is currently; "That is a very crucial point, that I have to search to find them where they are. So I must not think where they should be or where they ought to be, but where are they?" To discern where a supervisee is, Andersen indicated he might ask them, "How would you like to use our time together?" and "What would you like me to do in this meeting?" Such questions reflect Andersen's valuing of others and their perceptions of self.

Ideas About Working With Supervisees

We then turned our attention to asking Andersen to apply his ideas about the nature of human beings, language, and change and development to the practice of supervision. In applying his thoughts about language to working with supervisees, Andersen discussed how he observes a supervisee in order to discern which words have specific meaning for the supervisee. "Some of what the supervisee tells me appears to touch the person's self more than other words or if you talk about a certain passage in the therapy I can see they get moved." Andersen also suggested observing the physical movements made by a supervisee, as these may be signals to parts of the conversation that are important to the supervisee. Such physical movements may include restlessness, or a cough or laugh, or other mannerisms.

Once he observes a potentially significant word, Andersen mentioned he may "test" the word with the supervisee by asking her or him to talk more about that word. This would be one way to slow down or stop significant moments that would otherwise pass quickly. Supervisees may be having difficulty seeing and hearing options other than those they had first attempted in their work with a client, perhaps because a supervisee is experiencing fear, anger, sadness, or other limiting or constraining forces. In such a case, by "stopping the moment," the supervisee may be able to see and hear what at first she or he was unable to see and hear. As an example of such a situation, Andersen considered how to respond to a supervisee who said "I think I should be more structured in my therapy." Andersen suggested that the word "structured" be stopped and explored, perhaps by asking the supervisee, "Say more. What is it for you to be structured? What do you do when you try to be structured?"

Similar to the idea of stopping the moment at a point of significance for the supervisee, Andersen also described how he attempts to avoid interpreting what a supervisee is saying; "I try to listen to every word and avoid making up my meanings of a word I hear." Andersen gave the following example, edited by the authors, to illustrate a time when he felt he had not stayed with a person's language and may have become interpretive:

> One therapist wanted to have a consultation. She did some home visits and she used the words "there was so much noise going on that I was overwhelmed." And instead of sticking to the word "overwhelmed" and asking her to say more about this, I started to structure the reality by asking questions about how to organize the home visits differently. For example, I asked something like, "Do you think it might be a good idea to meet with the parents without the kids." And everything stopped. We got stuck. I should have stayed with the word "overwhelmed" and asked her to say more about this. "What made you become overwhelmed? What happens when you are overwhelmed? What do you think when you are overwhelmed?"

Much of Andersen's use of language, particularly his use of questions, attempts to broaden the perspective of the supervisee. So rather than being instructive or offering advice to supervisees (which may produce limiting change), Andersen asks supervisees questions that expand on what they have already said and done. Such questions may encourage supervisees to think about expanded or multiple ways of working with families. Examples of such questions include, What did you tell the family? How did that work? Have you had a chance to think of telling them in more than one way what they might do? Is this the only way to tell them what they might do or are there more ways to do this?

Another way that Andersen attempts to help supervisees broaden their perspectives is by asking questions that bring out the possible views of others. These other people might include coworkers and various family members with whom the supervisee is working. Questions that encourage thought about others' perspectives include, Are there particular things the family would like us to discuss in supervision? If the family had been here to hear our conversation, what might they be thinking? If you were to consult with your coworkers, what might they say could be discussed with the family?

Again in referring to the connection between language, meaning, and change, Andersen shared that it may be helpful to discuss with supervisees the variety of understandings that different family members may have of the same word or phrase. For example, Andersen described a client who was sad when she spoke of her growing independence from her family. When this woman was asked to "look into the word" *independence*, she replied that she saw loneliness. She was then asked what her mother would see in the word *independence*, and the woman said strength. Understanding that the same words may have different meanings to different people may help supervisees to expand their perspectives on how to be present with clients so that they might continue their thoughtfulness.

At times supervisees' perspectives may be limited such that they perceive it is difficult for them to work with a client. Andersen gave the example of a supervisee who was working with a family in which there was a man whom the supervisee viewed as angry and dangerous. Although she had been meeting with the family for two years, she had never met this man. In his conversation with the supervisee, Andersen noted that the man was perhaps excluded and alone. He asked the supervisee if she thought this man had feelings other than anger, and they discussed this man's possible feeling of sadness. Andersen then suggested that if someone were able to reach the sad side of the man so that side came forth more, maybe this man would be less dangerous. By gaining a different perspective of the man, the supervisee was able to meet with him; "How can I talk with a trainee such that they change their opinion of a person, such that they want to meet with the person? It is hard to meet with a person who is very dangerous and angry. But a lonely man, a sad man is easier to meet."

By helping supervisees broaden their perspectives, their possibilities for work with families may also be broadened; "That is my job, to be there such that a person can find his or her own endless possibilities." In doing this job, Andersen stated that he has to put away his standards and work from the supervisee's standards. For example, Andersen said that although he is not a strategic therapist, he would not try to change a strategic therapist to be less strategic. Rather, he would try to open up more possibilities for strategic therapy by asking questions such as, Is there more than one way to be strategic? What would fit you the best? What would fit the family the best?

When Andersen indicated that his job in supervision is to help a supervisee find his or her own endless possibilities, we wondered how he would work with a supervisee who asked for specific advice about how to proceed with a family. Andersen indicated that he would never tell a supervisee what he or she should do. Rather, he may share what he would do or he might offer several proposals from which the supervisee might choose. But to directly tell a supervisee what to do might limit the supervisee's possibilities for change and action.

In reviewing these thoughts on working with supervisees, the significance of Andersen's thinking about the nature of human beings, the importance of language, and change and development comes to the foreground. Supervisees, like all people, are constantly changing and preparing for their next steps. When preparing for these next steps, through the use of helpful language, supervisors can help supervisees expand their perspectives in ways that are not limiting but that encourage expansion and renewal.

The Use of Reflecting Teams for the Group Supervision of Counselors-in-Training: From the Authors' Experience

The use of reflecting teams as a form of group supervision of counselors may serve as an application of Andersen's premises about the nature of people, language, and the expansion of perspectives. In addition to being used with clients in counseling, as described earlier, the reflecting team process has been used as a means of group supervision for counselors-in-training. What follows is a description of the authors' experience with reflection and reflecting team supervision in a counselor education program, in counseling practicum classes in which the students were seeing families for counseling. The authors' experience has been strongly influenced by the work of staff members at the Brattleboro Family Institute (Davidson & Lussardi, 1991) and Prest, Darden, and Keller (1990), who have written of their use of reflecting teams in supervision.

At times the supervisor may for legal or therapeutic reasons need to be more directive in working with a supervisee even though reflecting team supervision may be used as a means for supervisees to discuss and reflect on their work with clients. To prepare for the reflecting team process, an interview dyad is formed, consisting of a student interviewee and an interviewer (the instructor or another student). The rest of the class members (usually four to six) serve as the reflecting team.

As described earlier in this chapter, the reflecting team process itself may consist of four steps:

- the interview dyad talks together about a family the interviewee is seeing for counseling;
- the reflecting team shares their thoughts about what they have heard from the interview dyad;
- the interview dyad responds to the reflecting team's reflections;
- the whole class (interview dyad and reflecting team) discusses the reflecting process they have just experienced.

These four steps are described in more detail in what follows.

In the first step of the reflecting team process, the interviewer talks with the interviewee for perhaps 10 to 20 minutes about a family the interviewee is seeing for counseling. During this conversation, the interview dyad sits facing each other in one corner of a classroom, separated from the rest of the class members who serve as the reflecting team (who are in another area of the same room). The interviewer and interviewee talk only to each other as the reflecting team members silently listen. Interviewers may choose to ask interviewees the following types of questions: What are your concerns about the clients you are working with? Where do you feel "stuck" in your work with this client? Where do you feel you are making progress with this client? That is, tell me where you see progress in your work with this client. How could the reflecting team be of help to you? Such questions are intended to provide the reflecting team with useful material on which to reflect and share comments. During this interview, the interviewee might show a portion of a videotaped counseling session with the family to further illustrate his or her concerns. Once the interviewee's concerns are expressed, the interviewer suggests that the reflecting team share their thoughts, which is the second step in the reflecting team process.

During this second step, the interview dyad quietly listens while the reflecting team members share their thoughts and questions about the interviewee and the interviewee's clients. The reflecting team sits in a circle and addresses fellow reflecting team members only; the reflecting team does not speak with the interview dyad. Reflecting team members are encouraged to reflect a multiplicity of views in a fashion that expands on the interviewee's strengths and possibilities for working with the client. These multiple views might include thoughts about human nature, about helpful language, and about change and development. For example, a reflecting team member in commenting on human nature, the constancy of change, and preparing for next steps, might inquire about steps already taken that have been helpful in counseling. Another team member might puzzle over possible meanings of a word or words that the supervisee had used. Both of these reflections could open space for change to occur. This time of reflection may vary from 10 to 30 minutes, until a reflecting team member or the interviewer suggests that the interview dyad discuss what they have heard from the reflecting team.

In the third step in the reflecting process, the interview dyad responds to the reflecting team's reflections, again with the interviewer and interviewee speaking only to each other. The interviewer may ask such questions as, What was significant to you about what the team shared? What did the team say that might offer some "next step?" What did the team say that seemed limiting or constraining?

As a final step, the whole class (interview dyad and reflecting team) may discuss the reflecting process they just experienced. Participants continue to share their thoughts about how to be reflective and helpful reflecting team members. At times attention is given to how to listen for changes that are occurring for the supervisee and to the multiplicity of ways supervisees and clients use language to discuss change.

This is one of many possible ways to adapt the use of reflecting teams to the group supervision of counselors. As Andersen (1995) noted, the only limit to our use of the reflecting process is our own inventiveness.

Concluding Thoughts

Perhaps some of Andersen's ideas are best summarized in a quote from his interview. When discussing his preference for talking with people rather than instructing them, Andersen said, "[rather than instruct someone] I would rather say, how can I be there such that the other person has a chance to think?"

The authors are grateful for the time that Tom Andersen spent with them sharing his thoughts. We hope that his ideas about people, language, and change and the application of these ideas to supervision will stimulate a change for the reader that expands and opens new possibilities in professional practice.

References

Andersen, T. (1987). The reflecting team: Dialogue and meta-dialogue in clinical work. *Family Process, 26*, 415–428.

Andersen, T. (1989). Back and forth and beyond. *Australian and New Zealand Journal of Family Therapy, 10*(2), 75–76.

Andersen, T. (Ed.). (1991). *The reflecting team: Dialogues and dialogues about the dialogues*. New York: Norton.

Andersen, T. (1992). Reflections on reflecting with families. In S. McNamee & K. J. Gergen (Eds.), *Therapy as social construction* (pp. 54–68). London: Sage.

Andersen, T. (1995). Reflecting processes; acts of informing and forming: You can borrow my eyes, but you must not take them away from me! In S. Friedman (Ed.), *The reflecting team in action: Collaborative practice in family therapy* (pp. 11–37). New York: Guilford Press.

Davidson, J., & Lussardi, D. J. (1991). Reflecting dialogues in supervision and training. In T. Andersen (Ed.), *The reflecting team: Dialogues and dialogues about the dialogues* (pp. 143–154). New York: Norton.

Prest, L. A., Darden, E. C., & Keller, J. F. (1990). "The fly on the wall" reflecting team supervision. *Journal of Marital and Family Therapy, 16*(3), 265–273.

7

Discovering a Choice of Lenses: A Postmodern Approach to Couple and Family Counselor Training

Ellen S. Amatea, PhD
Peter A. D. Sherrard, EdD
Silvia Echevarria Rafuls, PhD

Exhausted, Claudia takes a deep breath and begins to describe her recent session with the Gregory family to her clinical supervisor. It had been a nerve-wracking session with the Gregorys, a family composed of three little boys, ages 9, 7, and 5, and their 28-year-old mother, Sarah. This was the third time Claudia had seen the boys together with their mother for counseling, and she admitted that it always seemed to go the same way. "The boys enter the room as if shot from a cannon," she says. "Each heads toward a different shelf or cabinet, pulling out toys while their mother follows behind them, uttering orders in a soft, apologetic voice. Sarah tries to engage one of her boys in a game and doesn't seem to even notice when one of her sons climbs up on a bookshelf or the other pulls all the toys out of the cabinets."

Now with the session behind her, Claudia wants to think about what had happened. It had been a teeth-gritting hour, and she knows she has to do something different. But what would work? As she and her supervisor watch the videotape of the session to-

gether, she sees herself moving around the edges of the playroom picking up the toys the boys have pulled out of the cabinet and rushing over to protect the videocamera from falling as two of the boys hit each other with plastic bats. She knows she is feeling exasperated with Sarah for being so ineffectual with her sons. "It seems like each time I have seen a need for Sarah to direct her children to do or not do something and have told her to take charge, she has made excuses for the children's behavior rather than take a stand with them," Claudia says. "Look, here is where Tommy is starting to climb up on this tall bookcase. He can hurt himself! Did you notice, even here, I have to point out for Sarah to do something! She seems to be totally unaware of her need to take charge of the situation!" Claudia sighs. "What is wrong with this mother? Why won't she take charge of her children? I'm showing her what she could do! What is holding her back?" She catches herself as her supervisor gently asks: "What about you, what is holding you back?"

As she thinks about her supervisor's question, an answer flashes in her mind. She has been troubled by a recurring question during these meetings with the Gregorys: "Will these meetings really make a difference?" After all, the boys had been removed from their mother two years earlier when charges were made about the two older boys being sexually abused by one of her boyfriends. The three boys, each fathered by a different man, had been placed with a foster family who seemed to care deeply for them and had indicated an interest in adopting them. Yet their mother had continued to hope that she would get her boys back; she had moved in with her mother, gotten a minimum wage job and had faithfully followed the counseling and visitation schedule laid out by the child welfare authorities for the past two years. Claudia knew that a decision was pending as to whether the boys would be returned to their mother or continue in foster care. She thought about these little boys. They seemed angry with their mother and had told Sarah that even if they came to live with her, she (Sarah) could not "tell them what to do." Everyone seemed anxious to have things decided. Could that be why they were so rowdy and out of control when meeting with their mother? Could it be that Sarah, trying hard to have her sons like her, avoided any open shows of parental authority that might distance them from her? And what about Sarah's ability to care for them. Would she really be able to parent them effectively, or more important, protect them from the men in her life who might exploit them? They all—Claudia included—seemed to be living in a kind of limbo until the judge decided. How could she—a young, inexperienced family counselor—change the balance? And given the best interests of the children, should she change the balance?

The problem that faced the exhausted Claudia, that of figuring out how to help Sarah and her children, is faced by many counseling and social service professionals employed in children's mental health services. Examining the questions that Claudia asked herself about this family's situation and her role in it reveals a frame of reference about this mother's difficulties (and the appropriate clinical response) that is shared by the majority of America's social service workers and mental health professionals. This frame of reference, variously called a technical-rational, mechanistic, modernist, or positivistic worldview (Auerswald, 1987), assumes that the world in which we live, the world that contains the problems we try to solve, operates similarly to a machine. That is, everything has a predictable structure with fixed and movable parts, and a problem is viewed as an event that occurs as a result of a part malfunctioning. Thus if Sarah or her family is experiencing problems, it is a result of some faulty part; someone (e.g., Sarah) is not acting properly. Or someone has put too much pressure on certain members of the system who cannot bear the load, and thus the system breaks down. Solving problems within this epistemological perspective assumes that one must search for the part or parts that are damaged, weak, or missing and either fix them or replace them. Thus the task of the clinician is to discern who and what is to blame (e.g., a parent, a family, a judicial system) and then initiate action to correct the malfunction.

Although most of us are familiar with this modernist view of the nature of the world and the way it works, we may not be aware of how this worldview not only shapes what we know about our clients and their social worlds but also how we know it and how we decide to use the knowledge in formulating a course of action. The awareness of how our worldview shapes (and limits) our understanding is evoked when we are faced with alternative worldviews, each of which generates certain kinds of knowledge about clients and their social worlds while excluding the possibility of other knowledges ever being formed.

In this chapter, we describe some of the perceptual and conceptual shifts we have experienced in our ways of knowing and inquiring as, in response to the influence of postmodern thinking, we differentiate distinctively different epistemological lenses through which to construct our clients' worlds. We then present how we introduce our students and trainees to the use of these lenses in the design of particular training and supervision activities. Finally, we discuss the impact this awareness of a choice of lenses has on ourselves and our trainees.

Discovering a Choice of Lenses

As have so many clinicians and educators of clinicians, we have experienced a series of transforming moments in our understanding of and inquiry into the social worlds of clients, clinicians, and ourselves, which have generated significant influences on both our clinical practice and clinical training. In the 1970s our attention moved from viewing the individual client in isolation to viewing the client's behavior as relevant to the various systems in which he or she lives. This first shift, what Neill and Kniskern (1982) referred to as the move from "psyche to system," challenged us as clinicians and educators to contextualize our clients—noting the client's situation-in-life and how the client's behavior fit the client's network of relationships and social ecology. In the 1980s our thinking shifted further from viewing the designated system from the outside as an objective observer to acknowledging our position inside a designated system as a participant-observer. This second shift, what Keeney (1983) documented as the move from simple cybernetics to second-order cybernetics (or cybernetics of cybernetics), has challenged us to contextualize ourselves and to account for the impact our observations and stories have on both ourselves and on the human systems with which we are involved. In the 1990s, under the influence of postmodern ideas, our thinking is shifting again—from an either/or perspective to both/and, from universe to multiverse—in an effort to gain the benefits of double description and depth perception (Bateson, 1979). We now search for multiple accounts of the "stuff of life" in our search for differences that make a difference. The cumulative perspective emerging from these various shifts of consciousness promotes a change in our ideas about change—especially our ideas as to whom we should work with, how we think about the construction and reconstruction of reality, and how we position ourselves regarding that reality—a shift in epistemology (see Endnote).

G. Bateson (1977) believed that each of us—whether client, clinician, or educator of clinicians—formulates our own answer to what knowledge is and how we know it. He asserted that one cannot *not* have an epistemology: "You cannot claim to have no epistemology. Those who so claim have nothing but a bad epistemology. Every description you make is based upon, and contains implicitly, a theory of how to describe" (p. 147). Epistemology is, according to Bateson (1979), "always and inevitably personal. The point of the probe is always in the heart of the explorer; what is *my* answer to the question of knowing?" (p. 98).

So what is epistemology and what is its relevance in the training of marriage and family clinicians? Held and Pols (1985) suggested that two different meanings have been attributed to the concept of epistemology in the behavioral sciences literature: the first meaning addresses "the nature of knowledge" —both with *what* knowledge is as distinct, say, from mere belief or prejudice; and with *how* we know" (p. 510). By contrast, the second meaning "is more concerned with what we know (or think we know)," (p. 510) that is, with what philosophers call metaphysics or ontology: the inquiry into the nature of the world as it is.

Our interest is in the nature of knowledge, particularly, "the process of knowing, constructing and maintaining a world of experience" (Keeney, 1982, p. 165). By consciously reflecting on "how we know," we as clinicians and trainers of clinicians are attending to how we "edit" the universe and how we participate in the "social construction of reality" (Berger & Luckmann, 1966). "The fundamental act of epistemology is to draw a distinction—distinguishing an 'it' from the 'background' that is 'not it' (Keeney, 1982, p. 156). Bateson (1979) referred to this activity as "punctuation." A particular punctuation organizes or patterns events in a certain way:

> Punctuating or mapping a world follows from how an observer *chooses* to see....What we see is always a map, never the territory or thing in itself....In cybernetics, seeing a world follows from how we draw it. It is as if one's hand draws outlines on one's own retina. The process is recursive—what one draws, one sees, and what one sees, one draws. (Keeney, 1982, p. 157)

Thus, the act of punctuating, or drawing distinctions, involves everyone—mother and son, judge and defendant, counselor and client, supervisee and supervisor—in the construction and reconstruction of reality.

Each of the shifts of consciousness we have experienced since the 1970s we now recognize as choice points regarding punctuation. We stress these choice points, epistemological lenses, in our clinical training work. The first involves *focus and boundary* and designates the marking of the particular system that we make the subject of our statements such as the "self/other/context" distinction advanced by Satir (1972), where context includes both system and ecosystem (i.e., the cultural and geopolitical environment). We can focus on an individual, others in communication with that individual or with each other, the systems within which the event is taking place, or the various environments of the designated systems.

The second shift highlights *position and relationship*, the first-order and second-order cybernetic distinction advanced by Keeney (1982). We can take the position of observer or participant-observer. We can stand outside and/or inside the system(s) we are observing. Wiener (1948) believed that looking at the whole picture meant including self as participant-observer: "Essentially your ecosystem, your organism-plus-environment, is to be considered as a single circuit....and you're not really concerned with an input–output, but with the events within the bigger circuit, and you are part of the bigger circuit" (Brand, 1976, p. 37).

M. C. Bateson (1977) argued that the views from both positions (inside and outside) were significant and valuable, as evident in his observation regarding a projected study of dolphins that "there are at least *two levels* to be studied all the time, dolphin events, relationships, and meanings, and events, relationships, and meanings involving *scientist and dolphin*" (p. 72). The first level marks the scientist as observer; the second level references her or his participation and its impact on the event observed as well as the event's impact on the observer.

The third shift of consciousness we have experienced involves *inquiry and description*, and embodies the explanatory distinctions drawn by Dewey and Bentley (1949/1973) to differentiate among various realities. How do we attribute action and cause? To what (or whom) do we assign responsibility (or blame) for initiating action and creating outcomes? Dewey and Bentley (1949/1973) identified "three levels of organization and presentation of inquiry in the order of historical importance" (p. 107) and used hyphens to stress the significance of the verbal elements in the levels:

> *self-action*: where things are viewed as acting under their own powers,... *inter-action*: where thing is balanced against thing in causal interconnection,... and *trans-action*: where systems of description and naming are employed to deal with aspects and phases of action... such that no one [part] can be adequately specified apart from the specification of [the whole]. (p. 108)

Self-action asserts that the organism studied exhibits internal control and is acting under its own powers in generating and perpetuating intrasystemic regularities. "Self-action signifies behavior springing from the internal, pre-set, wound-up condition of a detached, organized entity, like a clock. The concepts of instinct and of the hereditary development of the organism are self-action concepts" (Papajohn & Speigel, 1975, p. 4).

By contrast both inter-action and trans-action assert that the organism studied is constantly subject to outside influences; however, each mode of inquiry highlights the significance of these influences differently. Inter-active inquiry "refers to the effect the behavior of organized, detached entities such as billiard balls or gas molecules has on each other" whereas trans-active inquiry "describes the interpenetration and mutual, reverberating, and reciprocal effects of processes that can no longer be considered organized, detachable entities" (Papajohn & Speigel, 1975, p. 5). Inter-action refers to acts and ideas that are viewed as if they were past occurrences, whereas trans-action refers "to the context of present experience, to that which is immediately at hand" (Speigel, 1971, p. 12). Thus inter-action refers to the type of inquiry that assumes that the various elements of a system have been adequately named and known prior to the start of inquiry so that attention is given only to what results from the action and reaction of the given elements on one another, whereas trans-active inquiry accepts descriptions of events as tentative and preliminary so that new descriptions of the aspects and phases of events may be freely made at any and all stages of inquiry. Inter-action treats elements as if they were static, whereas trans-action regards elements in continuous space-time where "thing is in action, and action is observable as thing" (Speigel, 1971, p. 25). Inter-action involves linear logical procedures, "split off and discontinuous with the present," whereas trans-active inquiry is circular, "proceeding from knowing to known and back, from one aspect of a system to another and then back to the first aspect" (Speigel, 1971, p. 26). These three modes of inquiry might be considered to roughly parallel the three levels of thinking described by postmodernists: that of premodern, modern, and postmodern thought. Each of these action modes of inquiry direct our attention to the construction of a particular "social reality" that generates very different causal explanations—all of which can be useful. Consider, for example, propositions advanced in quantum physics which assert that all being at the subatomic level can be described equally well either as solid particles (like so many minute billiard balls) or as waves (like the undulations of the surface of the sea). Neither description is really accurate on its own:

> both waves and particles are equally fundamental. Each is a way matter can manifest itself, and both together are what matter *is*. And while neither "state" is complete in itself, and both are necessary to give us a complete picture of reality, it turns out that we can never focus on both at once....Either we can measure the exact position of something like an electron when it manifests itself as a particle, or we can measure its momentum (its speed) when it expresses itself as a wave, but we can never measure both, exactly, at the same time. (Zohar, 1990, p. 26)

This is the nub of the Uncertainty Principle; although the wave and particle descriptions of being reveal its essential duality, they preclude each other because we can never focus on both at once. Nonetheless, we generate without either description at great peril. Similarly, it is in the recognition that there can be two or more legitimate descriptions of the same phenomena that we embrace the three modes of inquiry advanced by Dewey and Bentley (1973). By utilizing each mode, we seek "the difference that makes a difference" (Bateson, 1979, p. 68) in "changing our way of changing" (Keeney, 1982). After all, "it takes at least two somethings to create a difference" (Bateson, 1979, p. 68).

These shifts of consciousness now offer a variety of strategies we can use to generate transformations. We can change focus by redrawing the boundary that delimits the subject matter of our inquiry and regulates what is included in and/or excluded from our vision. We can change position by stepping into or out of the action addressed. We can change our mode of thinking by adopting first one, then another, of the modes of inquiry in order to generate differences that can make a difference. In each case, new possibilities emerge because we keep changing our way of thinking about changing (see Table 1).

TABLE 1
Epistemological Lenses

Focus and Boundary Lenses	Position and Relationship Lenses	Inquiry and Description Lenses
Designating the particular client system we choose to understand or make the focus of our attention such as the individual, others in communication with the individual and each other, the systems in which those interactional events take place, or the various environments of those systems.	Choosing the particular position we wish to take in observing and seeking to understand a system of interest. We can choose either to be an outside observer—standing outside of the situation we are observing—or view ourselves as a participant-observer—acknowledging the observer's impact on the event observed as well as the event's impact on the observer.	Understanding a system of interest using one of the following modes of inquiry to explain causality: self-active, inter-active, and trans-active. Self-active modes of inquiry explain things/people as acting under their own powers. Interactive modes of inquiry view things as acting in response to the actions and reactions of others in causally interconnected ways. Trans-active modes of inquiry view things as being influenced by actions and reactions occurring in the present and inseparably linked to the larger whole.

Significant benefits can accrue when we oscillate through the lenses (or strategies) described, benefits analogous to the "bonus" of depth perception gained from binocular vision. Just as one can choose among lenses of varying power on a microscope, so can a clinician or clinical educator choose among a variety of modes of description (i.e., epistemologies) when viewing the realities of clinical practice and training. And as we have stated elsewhere,

> Just as each microscopic lens can introduce the observer to realities not observed before, so can each epistemology introduce the clinician (or social scientist) to social realities not recognized before, social realities that often contradict each other. Furthermore, just as each microscopic lens can elicit an awareness that what one thought looked irrevocably one way, can, in fact, be seen another way, so can each epistemology elicit an awareness that the view of reality one has held as "true" may be alternated with another view, often contradictory with the first, which is equally convincing. This awareness arises as a benefit of "double description" (Bateson, 1979) and constitutes the essence of the ecosystemic revolution that has generated an epistemological framework synthesizing cybernetics, ecology, and systems theory. (Amatea & Sherrard, 1994, p. 7)

This discovery of a set of opposing truths reminds us that truth is a function of the "thought rules" (chosen from among alternatives) by which we construct the particular realities of our clinical practice and training. We invite you to join us in seeing and choosing more clearly the epistemological lenses by which each of us (as authors and educators) think and organize our clinical training activities. To this end, we discuss the basic goals around which our clinical training activities are organized and illustrate how these goals drive the specific training experiences we construct for our trainees. We want our trainees to be conscious of the clinical realities they are creating and being created by so we will describe the personal impact the recognition of this choice of lenses has on our trainees and on ourselves.

Introducing the Lenses: The Design of Training Experiences

We have chosen to design a series of training experiences for our students that we hope invites them to see themselves more as coparticipants in constructing an ongoing story of their own development of clinical competence and influence rather than as taking on the "right" way of thinking or of learning the "best" strategies. In this section we describe some of the ways we are working with these ideas in three different aspects of our training program: in our family therapy skills course, our community counseling course, and in our course on legal and ethical issues for family counseling practitioners. A central quality of these training experiences is our effort to use a wondering "what if/ what might be" stance for opening up our ways and our trainees' ways of thinking about their clients, themselves, and the larger political-clinical practice contexts in which they live and work. We hope that readers will find these ideas useful in eliciting new ways of thinking about their own work.

The Family Therapy Skills Course

"How could she—a young, inexperienced family counselor—change the balance?" This sentence not only describes Claudia's dilemma, it also reflects the experiences of most beginning family counselors and therapists. The concerns that go along with this stage of a therapist's development are captured well in Claudia's struggle with uncertainty and self-doubt as she works with the Gregory family. Underlying the struggle, however, is the more gripping and incessant question: "Am I competent enough to handle this situation?" If you think back to the time when you first encountered a family in a clinical setting, some of the questions that may have floated in your head during your first family session may have been, "What do I do now?" "How am I going to be able to manage all of their concerns and all that is going on in this room?" "Who is my client here?" and of course, the more existential, "What am I doing here?" These are some of the questions that students in the Family Therapy Skills Course find themselves asking as novice clinicians.

This course is designed with several objectives in mind. As a second-level course in family counseling and therapy it is designed to help students develop an expanded knowledge base of systemic theory and practice. The course offers students greater familiarity with theoretical tenets and models of family counseling and therapy by exposing them to a wide variety of literature that includes both classic and more current, cutting-edge publications. The course also introduces students to the practice of couple and family counseling through training that is provided in the department's Couple and Family Therapy Clinic. The graduate students enrolled in the course provide services to couples and families from the local community in this clinic. Students are supervised live in this clinical experience by licensed faculty. In order to meet both didactic and clinically based purposes, the course is divided into a class format for two hours and then an evening clinic format for another three and one-half hours. We focus on the activities that comprise the clinic training component throughout this section.

Although the Family Therapy Skills Course is required for marriage and family counseling students, students who enroll in the course vary greatly in terms of their interests, specialty areas (i.e., the M.Ed./Ed.S., Ph.D., or Ed.D. degree within the areas of marriage and family counseling, mental health counseling, and school counseling), and their level of clinical experience. This diversity of backgrounds and interests presents interesting challenges in the more practical issues related to clinic assignments and coordination (i.e., matching students with clients, supervisors with students, and students as co-counselors). Regardless of background or experience, every effort is made to provide students with a supportive learning environment. An atmosphere of support and respect through an appreciation of multiple perspectives and experiences is offered from the very beginning as part of this course. Through written material (i.e., syllabus, course guidelines, stated assumptions of supervision) and dialogue, students gain an idea of how they are to participate and how they can position themselves in their clinic involvement. Rather than viewing these guidelines as imposing rules or absolutes, they are offered to create an atmosphere of collegial collaboration, respect, and acceptance of one another, to downplay what could easily be foreseen as a highly competitive, performance-oriented environment. Guidelines for participation, which relate to individual and multiple perspectives, self-of-the-trainee issues, and ethical and legal considerations, exemplify some of the areas of practice that are addressed in these documents and in our dialogue throughout the semester. These guidelines are derived from assumptions about learning and clinical practice that are based on a reflexive process of exchange (i.e., the mutual, recursive influence that is shared by all who participate). Table 2 illustrates how these areas are highlighted within one of the central course documents students are first given. It encompasses our vision of the kind of clinical learning environment we attempt to develop with our students.

We discuss specific clinic experiences within the context of our previously mentioned epistemological lenses (i.e., focus and boundary, position and relationship, and inquiry and description), followed by a description of the impact that some of these experiences have had on participants.

TABLE 2

Behind the Mirror Etiquette, Supervision, and Musings for the Counselor/Therapist and Teams Family Therapy Clinic

1. Guidelines (or Rules) of Participation

A. The underlying premise in teamwork is collaboration. Your comments and observations are an integral part of this process. Therefore, expressions that are made, verbally and otherwise, may be commented on by other participants when dialogue occurs. For purposes of collaborative dialogue and respect toward trainees you observe, do not say anything behind the mirror that you would not say to the trainees yourself. Supervisors/team members may ask you to share or discuss your specific remarks as part of the collaborative supervisory process endorsed in this clinic.

B. Trainees and their teams should spend some time discussing supervisory and team-related functions, expectations, and needs.

- a. If you are part of a Co-counseling Team, discuss how you will work together and coordinate efforts with regard to functions, roles, purpose, theory, etc. in relation to your clients.
- b. As a Consulting Team Member, discuss (with team and trainee) your functions behind the mirror related to coordination of communication with trainees (i.e., types of call-ins that would be useful, messages, etc.) and how and when to provide feedback (i.e., during breaks, in-session, and/or post-session).
- c. Feedback to trainees (as a Team member) needs to be constructive, challenging, and given in ways that stretch the trainee professionally (and personally). Critical, negative, deficit-based feedback to trainees will not be permitted (just as it will not be permitted from trainees toward clients, or supervisors toward trainees).

2. Perspectives

A. Individual Perspective

- a. Challenge yourself to own your own comments and observations. Notice that what you observe about clients/trainees/team members is noticed that way because of your own uniqueness and your choice of lenses.

B. Multiple Perspectives

- a. We all have something to contribute regardless of professional development and experience.
- b. An integration of multiple perspectives is an important aspect of collaborative supervision.

3. Self-of-the-Trainee

A. Share to the extent that you feel comfortable. Feel free to say, “I don’t know right now” or “I want to skip that” to any question that you may be asked. However, keep in mind that the course instructor carries the burden of responsibility with regard to the counseling/therapy that is rendered and as such may request further explanation regarding matters that could directly jeopardize the well-being of clients in the clinic.

(continued)

TABLE 2 *(continued)*

B. When providing feedback and when interacting with others in the clinic, realize that your perceptions come from "your own stuff." Take note of what you notice and own it as your own.

C. We may deal with some self-of-the-trainee (trainee-centered) issues during our supervisory process only to the extent that it will assist you with your clinical work (e.g., working through "blind spots," stuck points related to your own issues, and awareness of your own resources, etc.). Our goal is not to provide you with counseling/therapy but to help you become aware of how these areas are interrelated. Any need to work through any of your own issues should be done with a counselor/therapist outside of the department. (Available resources can be discussed with course instructor.)

4. Ethical and Legal Considerations

A. Language and behavior can create a particular reality. I (course instructor/supervisor) will challenge and encourage you (and me) to examine language that is constraining or oppressive (i.e., pathology-based, disrespectful, stereotyped, or biased language toward others). This kind of language is pervasive and can occur sometimes without intent. You will be encouraged to bring challenging issues like these out for open discussion. The richness of experience and growth that such dialogue can potentially offer you will depend significantly on the extent to which you allow yourself to do this.

B. Any information shared during class and clinic is intended for participants only. It would be a serious ethical violation for any participant to discuss our work with any member outside the clinic group. You are bound to this confidentiality indefinitely—not merely for the time that our clinic participants will meet.

C. Finally, humor is a great resource. Humor can bring constructive change and relief. Use it respectfully.

Emphasizing Focus and Boundary by Viewing the Participants as a Community of Stakeholders

The two most important functions served by the Family Therapy Skills Course are defined by those who participate (i.e., the players) in the process. These include (a) the function of training students in family counseling and (b) the function of serving client-families who come in for clinic services. Generally, the participants include the clients seen in the clinic, the student trainees enrolled in the course, the supervisors, and the course instructor (who also serves as one of the supervisors and as the Clinic Coordinator for that semester). The live supervision and clinical focus featured in this course create a different context of learning beyond the traditional student–teacher hierarchy. Essentially, it is through clinical practice and supervision that trainees come to learn a great deal about family therapy and counseling. In their process of observation and working together as teams, students also provide each other with a context of learning beyond the usually experienced teacher–student context. Students learn from each other in their work together as clinicians, team members, and as observers of each others' counseling with clients. The nature of this process creates different training opportunities that are dependent on the students' experiences with clients and on their own development. Therefore, the impact of learning through the experiences that students have has great influence on the teaching that takes place as well.

The distinction between self, other, and context can be vitally important in this mutually informative process of exchange. Although the boundary between self and other may be more distinct for participants in the clinic, the boundary around context may not. Context implies the inclusion of the clinic system and its ecosystem and is usually determined by various environments that participants bring to our attention (e.g., client-related systems like health care, employment, schools, or university-related systems that impact us as students and faculty). The reflexive context of learning that results from assuming mutual responsibility for teaching one another through our clinical work creates the opportunity to make all of the participants stakeholders in this process we share as we learn about families and family counseling and therapy together. This has tremendous implications for the way the trainees, supervisors, and course instructor interact and how each chooses to define self in relation to the others in the clinic.

In our climate of reflexivity and collaboration, a resource-based growth-oriented perspective is generally encouraged and used in our supervision and evaluation of trainees. Growth areas are addressed in terms of strengths as well as areas that may need further work or refinement. Also, in terms of ensuring the quality of care of our clients, there is a shared understanding that there may be times when it may become necessary for a supervisor to take a more active role in the counseling process. This would only occur in situations that may involve harmful treatment of clients (normally unintended or rare) or in less intense circumstances when the trainee deviates far from therapeutic goals and purpose or is at a loss in terms of intervention.

Emphasizing Position and Relationship

One of the opportunities for trainees in the clinic is the experience of live supervision that provides a two-way connection between the trainee and clients in the counseling room and the supervisor and team members in the observation room. From a first-order/second-order perspective (Bateson, 1979), it would be difficult to remain an outside, nonparticipant observer within the live supervisory context. However, this does occur in situations when cancellations allow trainees to be observers of sessions with which they are not normally involved. For the most part though, the immediacy of the interaction and feedback in live supervision provides the students with a much more active participant-observer role in the therapeutic process. This second level, the second-order view, references how each one of us participates in the therapeutic process, how our participation impacts the therapeutic system, and in turn, how the therapeutic system impacts us as participants. In this case the boundary is drawn around all of us as whole rather than separating us as distinct parts from each other.

The exchange that occurs between the client, trainee, and team within our two-way supervisory context is well illustrated by our use of reflecting teams (Andersen, 1991). Trainees are exposed to the concept and use of reflecting teams almost immediately when they are introduced to live supervision at the very beginning of the semester. Many have never encountered the concept of live supervision, and so a reflecting team exercise is used to help orient them to the difference between what is experienced in the counseling room (from a client and trainee's perspective) and what is experienced in the observation room (from a team member's perspective). This is done by dividing the class into two groups. The first group is asked to convene in one of the therapy rooms while the other group observes them from the observation room. The first group is given the task of discussing some specific issues related to readings they are given regarding live supervision (Berger & Dammann, 1982; Piercy, Sprenkle, & Constantine, 1986; Smith, Smith, & Salts, 1991; Young, 1989–1990). The observing team is given the task of reflecting on what is said by the other group, behind the mirror and later in the room with the discussant group when both discuss live supervision. The roles are then reversed for each of the groups.

Later in the semester, trainees are required to read about reflecting teams (Andersen, 1987) and the Greek chorus (Papp, 1980). After a didactic presentation is given emphasizing Andersen's (1987) ideas of picture level, explanatory level, and alternative possibilities as a framework for organizing reflections, a role play is conducted utilizing one of our clinic families as an example. The class is divided into family members, therapist(s), and team members, and a reflecting team is constructed around family issues presented by the therapist(s). The team members are asked to construct reflections that are speculative about the client's view of change and its possible impact on them and their situation. This role play exercise has been helpful in introducing trainees to reflecting teams.

Throughout the semester, reflecting team conversations are implemented as they fit with the therapeutic process. For example, a client couple who had experienced tremendous changes in their conflictual, stuck marriage was able to move on to a discussion about more intimate issues related to their sexual relationship (an issue of concern presented early in counseling). All of a sudden as they spoke with the trainee, the husband alluded to his awareness of the team listening to the conversation about their sexual relationship (an issue of concern presented early in counseling.) With a striking mindfulness, the husband alluded to his awareness of the observation of the team listening to what he felt was a particularly sensitive topic of conversation for them, yet both went on with their discussion anyway. Even though the couple had met the team previously, this was a vulnerable enough issue for him that it presented heightened concern on his part. After the husband's statement, the team acknowledged his feelings of vulnerability behind the mirror and chose to use a reflecting team as one way to balance out his experience. Behind the mirror we followed this suggestion by discussing the couple in greater detail regarding all that they had been through together (i.e., previous sexual abuse experienced by both, substance abuse, family conflict) and how far they had come along. The fact that they had reached a point of being able to discuss intimacy issues as they intended to earlier on in their therapy was a sign of progress in our view. We wanted to convey our acknowledgement of this as progress and change, and we also wanted to provide them with some way to balance out their more vulnerable position within the supervisory structure of live supervision and observation. By having the couple and the trainee observe us from the observation room as we (the reflecting team) dialogued about the couple's courage and process of change, the scales of vulnerability became more even. By conducting our dialogue in front of them rather than privately behind the mirror as we usually did, our process was made more transparent to them, placing us in a vulnerable position just as they had been earlier. With their consent, the reflecting team proceeded and an extremely powerful experience occurred for all who participated in the process. During "wrap-up" that evening, all who had been a part of the experience discussed the reflecting team's conversation in terms of the impact we thought it had on the clients and therapist–client system, on us as team members, and on us as a whole (i.e., clients-therapist-team). In discussing how we arrived at some of the reflections that we offered the couple and their therapist, one of the outcomes we noticed was the tendency for some team members to split in terms of gender when we spoke of their progress and issues, while other team members incorporated both. As it turned out, even though (our perception of) the husband's vulnerabilities led us to use a reflecting team, both partners needed to be included in our reflections in order to provide the couple with a balanced experience. The therapist reported that behind the mirror the couple was quite taken by the comments about them and their progress and were surprised to find out that this was the way we talked about them as a team.

Emphasizing Inquiry and Description

The three action modes of inquiry that were described earlier, self-action (initiative that emanates from self), inter-action (initiative that occurs as a response to the initiative of another), and trans-action (initiative as a function of reciprocal patterns of process and structure that constrain the action) provide trainees in the Family Therapy Skills Course with a third way to view their experiences. This particular lens helps trainees interpret and understand how all of the participants come together as part of the clinic process (i.e., what we do together as trainers and trainees during our evening clinic).

Generally, a trainee's ability to appreciate and understand his or her position along all three modes depends greatly on the trainee's integration and use of systems thinking, level of comfort as a clinician, and ability to trust in the other participants and in the process we share in. Trainees who are predominantly self-active in their orientation toward others are generally more performance-conscious and less able to relax and to trust in the process. Experiences along the continuum vary from those who have difficulty moving beyond a guarded self-active stance to those who embrace a linear stimulus–response perspective (interactive) to those who are able to shift significantly throughout the semester to a circular, trans-active stance that is jointly constructed and communal in nature (and has been known to transcend the bounds of the course and the semester for those who partake of the experience). In other words, ties that are established by trainees through trans-active experiences are known to remain rather strong and cohesive as trainees continue with their programs and clinical training.

Our understanding of a trainee's mode of inquiry and how that translates into an approach with others is derived from observing (a) the trainee's behavior with clients, supervisors, and other trainees and (b) the reflections that trainees write about themselves and their experiences in the journal entries they are required to keep from week to week. We provide an example of a shift from self-active to inter-active and trans-active inquiry with the aid of some actual excerpts taken from a former trainee's journal who consented to have the authors use some of her entries to illustrate her shift in thinking. This particular trainee, whom we refer to as W, was paired with another trainee throughout the semester, whom we refer to as J, and both were supervised by N. After seeing the family for the first time in session, W wrote in her journal how she felt like a newcomer to what she perceived was an already established therapist-supervisor team because N had supervised J in another agency before (self-active focus). She questioned her position and skills when she noticed that she thought differently about the client-family than they did.

> I went into the session with the belief that the best thing to do was probably the only thing I knew how to do—establish rapport, build trust, and build a therapeutic relationship. Very early in the session, I began to feel very inadequate—as though this "plan" was really not enough. I felt as though there were certain rules that J and N knew, but I did not know. [While W already felt sensitive to their previous connection, she heard N saying "good job" to J and she continues]... I hardly participated the rest of the time....Of course I felt reprimanded, and N's comment would only reinforce this feeling. I guess at this point I felt that I was supposed to be doing things that I did not want to do or know how to do.

Interestingly, toward the end of this same entry, the trainee revealed a shift toward a trans-active focus as she checked out other trainees' reactions toward her when she came back to the observation room for the intrasession break. Her trans-active focus freed her to move on to participate in the rest of the discussion the group had about the family and to benefit from their support. She wrote,

> In closing, I must finally get to my most memorable experience last week. It says a lot of things about this program and a lot of things about the family course. During the session as noted, I felt I was doing a really bad job. Naturally, I wasn't looking forward to debrief, but I gave myself instructions on how to look and act, and proceeded to enter the room. When I sat down I began to look at face after face. [Looking at the two she suspected would judge her more harshly she goes on] there was nothing in their faces to indicate that I had failed. Good. The toughest ones were over. [Looking at the instructor's

> face she writes] Piece of cake… and there was nothing but the same old depth of kindness and genuine caring that told me I was fine. I looked carefully at everyone—one by one. And there was nothing negative or questioning or even avoidant on [she names each individual in the rest of the group] faces. I was very attendant to the situation, so I could begin to feel myself recovering rapidly—it was not just emotional but physical and cognitive too. Very quickly I was not only feeling okay, but confident. I participated in the discussion and left feeling very good.

As this excerpt shows, the trans-active stance enabled her to benefit from the trust and acceptance from others she did not expect but nonetheless recognized. This allowed her to be a collaborative participant in a process of learning rather than a defended and threatened observer of her therapeutic process with her own clients. Similarly, there are many additional examples that could be cited. The rewards are plenty and the costs are generally few. The impact on trainees, supervisors, and instructors covers a full range of possibilities. Excerpts from other journal entries illustrate these well.

> After these sessions I feel much better about my prospects of being a therapist. I believe real success in anything takes hard, long work.... I cannot imagine leaving the program without having ever learned systems thinking. It is the most exciting and life-enhancing experience.
>
> I have grown to a point that helping the family is the main goal, and to the point that success is OUR success. Of course the overwhelming desire to be a good counselor and appear competent to peers and supervisors is still a big factor. But coming to know and like J [her co-counselor] and N [her supervisor] has made me comfortable with the fact that this is a group effort, not three individual ones. I know I have grown so much from this experience, and this is just one of the manifestations.
>
> This has been an interesting semester for me. In some ways I felt like I did my very first semester—feeling insecure and unsure. In my own personal growth this semester I learned that I have a tendency to try to do things on my own. I am not used to asking for or getting help or doing things with other people. I have a tendency to ride situations out without stopping and asking for help or clarification. I have begun the process of sharing my life "with" my fiancee and now with W [her co-counselor] and N [her supervisor]. I learned from not knowing how or when to share with them. Now I feel more ready to open up and give feedback etc….

With experiences like these, it is rewarding to know that the Family Therapy Skills Course can provide trainees with both personal and professional growth and satisfaction. It becomes apparent that somehow what the students have experienced has made a difference both in their experience of themselves and with those they will see in counseling.

The Counseling in the Community Course

Far too often, mental health professionals like Claudia, the counselor depicted in the opening case vignette, may work in organizational or clinical practice contexts where there are conflicting agendas inherent in particular requests for help. Should Claudia's goal be to assist Sarah in learning how to care for her children in a way that satisfies the legal system, or is Claudia's goal to protect the children from their mother and to expedite the legal decision to award the children to a foster family? Is Claudia's time with Sarah and her children to be devoted to helping the mother and children improve their relationships, is the focus to be on assessing the mother's and sons' capacities for relating, or is Claudia to merely serve as a "family-sitter" for the mother–child visitations? Whose interests are to be served? How are decisions made as to what type of services should be provided? How are such conflicting agendas to be resolved?

Not only do clinicians frequently find their role and function regarding their clients unclearly defined or in conflict with their own beliefs and values, they may also discover that the avenues for clarifying and restructuring these clinical roles and functions within their clinical practice contexts are shrouded in mystery. Who needs to hear about these conflicting role demands that Claudia is experiencing? How might Claudia bring her experience to light with other members of her work context in a manner that can serve to generate ideas as to alternative ways of responding to cases of this sort and clarify the potential gains and losses for the organization when pursuing these various pathways? Often mental health professionals may feel that they cannot speak out about such constraints; particularly when they fear that their position or livelihood would be threatened if decisions by those higher up in the administration of their agency are questioned. So they operate as if others outside of themselves and their clients are making the "big" decisions that shape their lives, which reflects the inter-active mode of explanation. Such beliefs and actions can lead mental health professionals to feel victimized, angry, fearful, and powerless, unable to act in their own or their clients' behalf. This may result in clinicians attempting either to deny or distance themselves from these inherent conflicts in organizational goals and values. They may blame certain members of the organization or the larger sociopolitical context for these circumstances and form coalitions where they think in "us against them" terms and in which they speak openly about their concerns only with their allies while presenting a carefully defended position when dealing with their opposition.

Because the "rules" for relating in many clinical practice contexts may constrain mental health professionals to respond in either an angry and closed off style or in a helpless and defeated style in dealing with such conflicts inherent in the larger organizational and political context in which they work, we believe it is essential that our students develop an early warning system. Therefore, we invite them to change their mode of inquiry (a) to anticipate the larger systems in which they will operate as counseling practitioners and to appreciate the ways in which their own beliefs and practices shape and are shaped by the larger system of beliefs and relationships characterizing these clinical practice contexts; (b) to examine the larger sociopolitical context in which their clinical practice is embedded together with its demands for change and adaptation and to review the strategies by which clinical practice contexts or organizations try to negotiate change; and (c) to explore strategies for introducing change into the beliefs and actions of coparticipants in one's work system and clinical practice context and to experiment with one such strategy in a practice setting.

The community counseling course, a mandatory one-semester course taught to second-year master's level students, is the context in which these goals are addressed. This course highlights our interest in the focus and boundary trainees choose to emphasize by inviting them to consider how practitioners "draw the boundary" as to whom they include as members of the systems of interest that influence their transactions with their clients. Our interest in the position and relationship of the practitioner in the therapeutic process is emphasized by asking students to examine the stories and beliefs about the valued goals, role, and strategies inherent in different clinical practice contexts. Their inquiry leads them to discover how beliefs and practices develop as a function of acculturation and socialization into a specific profession and a specific organizational culture, and how these beliefs influence choices regarding the target of clinical examination and intervention.

The narrative therapy process formulated by Michael White and David Epston (White & Epston, 1992) served as a model for the design of exercises and activities in this course. White and Epston assume that each of us is the custodian of a succession of stories that organize the picture we have of ourselves and the larger world, including a personal, gender, community, class, and cultural story. White and Epston (1992) wrote of this power of narrative to generate meaning and value:

> The idea that it is the meaning which persons attribute to their experience that is constitutive of the person's lives has encouraged social scientists to explore the nature of the frames that facilitate the interpretation of experience. Many of these social scientists have proposed that it is the narrative or story that provides the primary frame for this interpretation, for the activity of meaning making; that it is through the narratives that persons have about their own lives and the lives of others that they make sense of their experience. Not only do these stories determine the meaning that persons give to experience, it is argued, but these stories also largely determine which aspect of experience persons select out for expression, and, as well, inasmuch as action is prefigured on meaning making, these stories determine real effects in terms of shaping of persons' lives. (pp. 27–29)

Thus not only do we as clinicians participate in the stories of others, but others participate in our story. Furthermore, some of these stories are not necessarily in our best interest; these stories may need to be re-storied differently.

The course begins with a personal vision exercise designed to help students articulate their expectations as to the type of role they hope to play in their clinical practice contexts and their concerns as to type of role they fear they may play in their work contexts. First, students are asked to imagine in great detail a day 5 to 10 years in the future and to write a story as to how their life will be in the various arenas in which they perform. Students are then asked to write their story of current reality—a story that usually consists of current beliefs authored by themselves and others as to how organizations function and how professionals must operate in them to survive. The following set of questions are adapted from some formulated by Parry and Doan (1994) and can be useful in eliciting this second view.

1. What is my story of current reality (e.g., in a specific setting such as working in a community mental health center, in a group private practice, or in a large corporate managed care setting)?
2. Where did this story come from and who wrote it?
3. What role does it have me playing?
4. What supporting roles does this story need others to play in order for it to exist?

We recognize that our stories of our future lives and of current reality are shaped by larger narratives and meanings in our culture, that "we exist in some story larger than ourselves" (Parry & Doan, 1994, p. 50); therefore we find it useful to compare these stories and to identify the dominant central themes in them that may have the power to constrain or support our thinking and action as clinicians. What are these larger narratives? Mair (1988) responds: "We inhabit the great stories of our culture. We live through stories. We are lived by stories of our race and place. It is this enveloping and constituting function of stories that is especially important to understand more fully" (p. 127). Howard (1991) agrees: "The young learn to tell the dominant stories of their cultural group—be these stories scientific, civic, moral, mathematical, religious, historical, racial or political in nature" (p. 190).

Along with our students, we try to note those larger themes and stories that shape our current story of reality in our effort to create an alternative story that allows all of us to assume a more positive and empowering role within the context of clinical practice and various sociopolitical spheres of action. Often students view current reality as static and unchanging, view themselves as being outside of the circle of influence, and view others as being more experienced and knowledgeable than they. These themes are tied to larger themes of gender identity (e.g., that women have less of a voice than do men and thus their experience is of less value); of professional identity (e.g., to be an effective healer one should not think in terms of material, bottom-line outcomes); or of social tradition and history (e.g., that society should take care of its poor and not hold them responsible for their own care). We ask questions that invite inquiry into these themes: "What larger themes in your stories of current reality can you identify—themes concerning race, gender, social class, professional tradition—which inform your current reality story?" " Which of these support your vision story?" "How might they need to be changed, or are there different themes you would use?" We believe that such examination of hidden stories in the "way things are" in a human service organization or larger professional "family" reveals some of the unchallenged beliefs that powerfully influence our current actions and thinking, and also facilitates decisions as to what current beliefs might need to be more carefully examined, challenged, or changed.

A subsequent set of activities is designed to help students experiment with the possible various lenses associated with different modes of explaining and interpreting the reality of their clinical practice context. The *change project proposal* invites students to select a specific issue in a clinical practice setting with which they have some familiarity and to track the story of this issue (what it is, how it developed, and how it has been responded to). They are asked to create several possible alternative stories (i.e., descriptions of the issue and explanations as to its cause and necessary cure or solution) and to pay particular attention to how their own thinking about this issue changes. Next, we encourage our students to think about how they might participate in a cooperative effort with other members of this system who may be stuck in the problem with them; how can they collaborate in creating a different story about life with this problem or issue?

The following is a sampling of questions used in the first phase of the project to elicit multiple descriptions of a problem and its "life":

1. If, instead of viewing this problem as happening because someone mishandled it (i.e., screwed up), I saw it as a difficulty we were stuck in because we did not know how to see the longer term patterns of action and reaction of which this issue is a part, how would my story about this difficulty change?
2. If, instead of seeing the people involved in this difficulty as stubborn, resistant, or self-serving, I saw them as being stuck in a story of being afraid (of being wrong, being blamed, making a mistake), how would my story about these persons and their contribution to this difficulty change?
3. If I were more sensitive to each persons' perspectives on and experiences with this difficulty, and less tightly bound to just seeing my own perspective, what might I notice that has gone unnoticed before?
4. How am I making sense of this issue and the life of the organization around it which is different from the way others see it? What factors or influences or beliefs may have led to this view that I need to consider?

Senge and his associates (Senge, 1990; Senge, Roberts, Ross, Smith, & Kleiner, 1994) suggested that organizational problems might be more effectively viewed not as one-time crises, personal mishandlings, or problematic sequences of actions, but instead as part of a larger set of interrelated patterns of actions that trigger each other's development (i.e., "grow" each other) as a result of certain "mental models" or stories or beliefs that members of an organization hold. Following Senge and associates, students are asked to consider how the varied perspectives of members involved in the problem generate a larger system story that reveals certain underlying dominant beliefs or mental models about how the organization needs to run in order to survive. These survival stories parallel the survival stories of individuals in that they may contain outdated beliefs about how to deal with threatening situations. In creating each new view or story about the life of a difficulty, students are invited to think about how they might build a story with those involved in a way that helps them effectively "step outside the old story" by externalizing the problem (White & Epston, 1992) and begin to create an alternative story of life without the problem.

Commenting on the impact of class activities that allowed her to discover her own mental model of an organizational dilemma prior to considering different ways of storying about it, one student wrote,

> I find I am learning how I might tell the story of a situation without blaming, and as I've triedto do this more, I can actually see how a system's problems were growing themselves within a particular structure and without one particular culprit. It also became apparent that the process of how I arrived at the story would be helpful to share as it could be a way to get feedback and input as to the different actions or perceptions that affect the situation we feel stuck in.

As students are introduced by means of these activities to ways of working focused on issues in the larger organizational or sociopolitical contexts of which they are a part, they begin to recognize that they have a choice of interpreting their organizational context and role differently. This was demonstrated in the comments of one student who wrote,

> I believe that operating from the context of the ideas we've addressed in this class will be an empowering stance both for me and for those with whom I interact. I imagine myself assuming a posture in which I ask: How can we rewrite the narrative so that we focus on what is resourceful and resilient about us and our problem? What contextual frameworks can we name, and thereby interact with consciously rather than feeling like we are being controlled or victimed by our circumstances? These are strong messages about how we (those involved in a process or problem) interact with ourselves and our environment.

Finally, the class activities help students become aware of their potential influence on the organizational context. One student reported,

> One of the greatest effects of this class on me is that I can more easily visualize how my ideas may impact others and who and what is creating them to begin with. The thing I have to struggle hardest with is my own strong feelings about some things I feel pretty powerful at times to make changes. But sometimes, I feel I do not want to be a "change agent" when I have an acute case of indignation. Noticing when I feel this way and considering what mental models may be shackling my thinking is useful in helping me rethink my position.

Such feedback suggests that trainees have begun to embrace these new ways of thinking and working, admitting they find them a comforting alternative to either denying the existence of difficulties in their clinical practice context or dreading that they have little control to do something about them.

The Ethical, Legal and Professional Issues Course

As Claudia reflects on her reaction to her clients, she faces a multitude of value questions that have serious ethical importance. For example, what model of parenting does she espouse? What model does the mother espouse? What values drive each of these models? What is Claudia's obligation to the mother? To the boys? To the legal system? To the profession? To herself?

The Ethical, Legal and Professional Issues course is designed to help students face these questions and others like them. Students are asked to consider how the focus and boundary of their clinical and professional efforts and obligations shapes their definition of *client* (and vice versa). They examine the ethical implications of their choice of position and relationship regarding their clients, particularly the ethical implications of their degree of involvement with clients. And they explore the varieties of ethical discourse that are generated by the three modes of inquiry and description.

The course design provides a series of curricular experiences that invite students to follow the experiential learning cycle advanced by Kolb (1984): Students focus on a shared *concrete experience*, generate a series of *observations* based on those experiences, and discipline their observations by organizing them into various *abstract conceptualizations*, which lead to possible courses of action whose consequences can be tested (i.e., *active experimentation*) in both imagined and real scenarios. The seven headings below identify the stated goals of the course, each of which is followed by a brief outline of some of the activities (i.e., curricular experiences) used to help students accomplish these goals.

1. *Stimulating the moral imagination:* The class begins when students view excerpts from the PBS film *Facing Evil*, produced by Bill Moyers (1994). Students are invited to share their responses to the film and to think about some of the questions raised by the film, such as, What is evil? What is good? How do we know? Of what use are conversations about good and evil? How does human cruelty influence our understanding of human goodness? What does it take to do the good? What if someone (important) disagrees with our conception of the good? What is the cost of "goodness" (and "badness")?

After considerable discussion of the issues raised by the film, five student teams are formed, each of which is assigned a chapter (either chapter 3, 5, 6, 8, or 9) from the book, *Some Do Care* (Colby & Damon, 1992). These teams write a three-page summary of the "moral exemplar" described in the chapter and lead a class discussion on the issues inherent in the exemplar's life. In addition students are invited to complete a series of inventories, such as the Altruism Quiz (Hunt, 1990), the Ethical Beliefs and Values Survey (Sherry, Teschendorf, Anderson, & Guzman, 1991), and the Rokeach Values Survey (Rokeach, 1973). They are then invited to compare their responses to published norms and to discuss their thoughts about comparisons in class, asking such questions as, What have I learned? What surprises me? To what do I want to give more thought? What do I want to change?

2. *Becoming more aware of how personal biases and values influence one's conceptualizations and interventions:* After completing the moral exemplar reports, students are asked to seek out, interview, and report in writing on someone whom they consider a moral exemplar (following the interview guidelines in Colby & Damon, 1992). These reports are presented and discussed in class, with an emphasis on what students have learned from these interviews about the relationship between ethical inquiry and moral imperative and about their own personal aspirations and commitments. Several students wrote about a parent or relative whom they admired and wished to emulate. One student interviewed and wrote the following about a campus clergyman who had great influence on her during her undergraduate years:

> I remember him first in Jesus sandals, looking like a gnome with his mid-chest beard and chin-length hair, all mussed up and greying. He made the gospels sound like music, his lyrical voice pacing a cadence that Americans can't reproduce. He's an Irishman, a good Catholic by upbringing and seminary training, and a hippie at heart. He's an ordinary man, living the simple paradoxes of a life filled with introspection and social action. In the fiber of this man is an ethical structure that requires daily life to be filled with care and compassion. Personal honesty balanced with commitment to enduring ideals...I learned about joy and reckless affairs with ideas that grew out of Paul Tillich's head and Carol Gilligan's early work. Bernie was fondly accused by the interreligious council in the community, of raising Francis of Assisi and Clair beyond sainthood. Why would sixty or seventy college students lie around on the floor to watch *Brother Sun, Sister Moon*, and then dialogue about its relevance for a string of gatherings in its wake? Bernie made it believable. How did he do that? He lived like Francis. He still does. (Krueger-Casper, 1995)

Another student followed the suggestion of a friend and interviewed a 62-year-old stranger who impressed her with an admirable generosity of spirit and action:

> Barbara spends many hours a week at Good Samaritan Nursing Home and Retirement Village. It began several years ago when she decided to have an early morning breakfast at the coffee shop located in the Village. She noticed how sad and depressed some of the people looked and invited a few of them to sit at her table. She continued to have early morning breakfasts there. Before long her table was overflowing with 18 or 20 other people who came to regard this early morning gathering as the "Breakfast Club." As she listened to their stories she was shocked and saddened to hear how so many had little or no contact with their families. Often their own children lived far away or rarely visited. She became aware of their needs and felt compelled to do what she could to help. Frequently she takes residents to doctor's appointments. She often takes in food, or runs errands that need immediate attention. Sometimes she washes their clothes because the service provided is not always satisfactory. On numerous occasion she has assisted residents with their legal concerns, making sure their papers and documents were in order. On special occasions she remembers these people with birthday cakes, flowers for Easter and Mother's Day, and little gifts for Christmas. Many of the residents have put her name on emergency contact forms. It is not unusual for a physician to call and request her help with a resident who gets confused with medical instructions. Most importantly, Barbara has helped reunite some of the residents with estranged family members. Word quickly spread about this caring person who is willing to do so much. She sometimes receives calls to assist those she has never met. For all the time and energy she spends, she refuses to accept payment from these people...I felt privileged to be able to speak with this incredible lady. My life is somehow richer. I have been inspired by her unselfishness. (Politano, 1995)

3. *Facilitating the continued development of skills necessary to recognizing, analyzing, and resolving (where possible) ethical/moral dilemmas:* Students are now introduced to relevant selected writings on ethical inquiry (Huber, 1994; Kitchener, 1984, 1986), to the American Association for Marriage and Family Therapy and American Counseling Association ethical codes, and to relevant Florida legal statutes. They are given eight ethical dilemmas to analyze using the professional codes of ethics, the Kitchener principles, the known legal statutes, and their own sense of moral imperative. Their responses to these dilemmas are compared and challenged in subsequent discussion as they have opportunity to test their conceptualizations in ethical debate.

4. *Eliciting a sense of moral imperative and moral action in both personal and professional contexts;* and

5. *Helping each participant to tolerate the ambiguity inherent in disagreements about ethical/moral aims and purposes:* Students are invited to present to the class their own professional ethical dilemmas together with their case for an ethically informed course of action. After initial discussion of a case, we invoke a procedure designed to create a sense of the ecosystemic force field that constrains ethical discourse (Sherrard, Lord, Lord, & Pritchard, 1991) and exemplifies the social constructionist (Berger & Luckmann, 1966; McNamee & Gergen, 1992) and social conflict (Coser, 1956; Loder, 1989; Sennett, 1970) orientation of the instructor. The student presenting the dilemma identifies the "voices" relevant to the dilemma (as she or he sees it) and various class members articulate those voices and create arguments for a course of action compatible with the unique perspectives of each voice. Class members may add additional voices (by sitting in the available "empty chair") as the dialogue gains momentum and it becomes clear that a perspective is missing. The presenter asks questions, clarifies, listens, and argues until he or she feels the need to rest (i.e., the "pause" in creativity thinking), or until a sense of clarity and direction emerges. Students have been enthusiastic about the process because it externalizes the immobilizing debate in their head and allows them to experience the ethical and social force field as a constraint (rather than restraint) that "disciplines" viable courses of action. The approach is particularly helpful in the complicated "right vs. right" (Kidder, 1995) dilemmas so common today.

6. *Advancing the likelihood of ethical and moral conduct in carrying out one's present and future personal and professional activities and reducing the likelihood of unethical/immoral conduct;* and

7. *Enhancing the prospect for intelligent compassion when confronting ethical/moral indiscretion(s):* These two goals point to future patterns of thought and action. By identifying and gaining knowledge about moral exemplars who can serve as role models, by identifying and exploring personal biases and values, by analyzing the ethical dilemmas inherent in selected cases, and by struggling with the "voices" that compete for influence, we hope that both student and instructor will be better prepared to face the ethical challenges of the future with courage and conviction. To this end, the instructor serves as "gatekeeper and mirror, disturber and comforter, lighthouse and mystic in the fog that is sometimes the best measure and process of education" (M. Connelly, personal

communication, 1995). The instructor shapes the climate of discourse and risks the same vulnerabilities asked of the students, for in the ever evolving moral imagination, each of our preferences for focus, mode of inquiry, and position are continuously subject to scrutiny. The course elicits vigorous participation among the students and there is considerable evidence of deep reflection. Students were invited to write a paragraph or two at the end of the semester highlighting class experiences that were significant too them. One student summarized the impact of class activities and classroom climate with these words:

> In learning the ethical and legal considerations in marriage and family therapy, the instructor introduced us to ethical cases and chose two modes of exploring them. First, he provided us with ethical cases and a written exercise to address ethical and legal issues. Next, through an oral exercise in class, one person presented a case and several others in the class presented Kitchener's ethical principles. It created a dynamic interaction which externalized the decision-making process and allowed us to examine it more closely. For me, the process was exciting and creative. Aspects of the dilemmas I may have missed were brought to life and helped me to consider my own thought process. Exercises such as these sparked ongoing discussions and a sense of sharing and community that was felt the minute we walked through the door. Many of my classmates and I remarked how lucky we were to have had such a valuable experience and felt inspired to create this sense of belongingness in other professional arenas.

Another student addressed trans-active patterns essential to personal safety and elective growth:

> The issues defined in class and in assigned readings were appropriate materials relating to the laws and ethics of marriage and family counseling. Understanding these issues was the beginning of an intricate process of growth and learning. Much more was considered than what was found on the surface; in printed words, laws and codes. Dilemmas were examined which touched the very core of who we were. Such things could not have been examined in the traditional classroom where information is spoon fed and reciprocally regurgitated for the desired grade. Scores and grades are at best a sterile representation of what has been presented, what has been learned, and what changes have taken place. Questions and dilemmas which are at the core of learning must come forth in an environment where all of the facets can be examined and pondered. Students must feel a sense of safety in order to share their beliefs, questions, and understandings without fear of negative judgement or ridicule. The instructor provided us with such an environment where all the possibilities could

be explored. It was a place where we could consider our personal viewpoints, our frustrations, our idealism, and our newly discovered awarenesses. We were challenged as well as validated as we plunged into the depths of the material. And, we were greatly rewarded as we began to see growth within ourselves and others in the class. This growth represented a heightened awareness of the complexities of ethical, moral, and legal dilemmas and of the responsibilities we carry in our roles as counselors and therapists.

Impacts on Faculty and Students

We assume that our selection of the epistemological lenses (or thought rules) by which we construct the particular reality of our clinical practice and training not only signals our beliefs as to whom we focus on, but also whom we hold accountable for the world in its present state and how we function in relation to them. When we (and our students) stand outside the client systems we seek to influence, it is often easier to assess how larger systems (such as the courts or the welfare system) are influencing client behavior, and we can more easily hold those systems accountable for their impact. However, when we step into the picture as participants, we face how the meanings we give to clients and counselors (such as Sarah and Claudia) take on a life of their own and lead to unexpected outcomes. Accountability becomes more complex than we could ever imagine from the outside. The observer changes what is observed through the very act of observing, and the act of observing changes the observer. This is the reciprocal and recursive nature of influence.

It is this recognition that drives the changes in our training program in couple and family counseling. We highlight the lenses of focus and boundary, position and relationship, and inquiry and description in order to invite our students to consciously participate in the social construction of reality (i.e., "what we cannot wish away," Berger & Luckmann, 1966).

The process of developing an awareness of the alternative sets of lenses, or thought rules (i.e., of focus, position, and mode of inquiry or explanation), by which we can construct our clinical practice is fraught with a number of challenges. First, having no one "right lens"—no one proper way to operate clinically—creates a level of tension and uncertainty that beginning clinicians often find overwhelming. The idea that there is a correct way to see things creates the impression that one really knows how things work. However, this certainty often comes with a price; neither the clinician nor the various members of the client system learn to listen to their own good advice (or to their own problematic advice). Learning to perceive and think out loud together—in the academic and clinical aspects of the training program—about what each one is experiencing (rather than just assert one reality) is a radical departure from the way in which most counselor education has been structured. We have highlighted a limited student response to perceiving and thinking consensually with other members of the systems of interest, and this response is enthusiastic, thoughtful, and compelling.

Rather than consider the relative strengths and constraints of these thought rules in an effort to discover the best one, we believe that these lenses can be used in a complementary fashion shifting from one to another to generate "double description" (Bateson, 1979) of that which is observed. For example, in choosing the lens of position, Andersen (1991) observed that

> It is easier to take a second order (participant observer) view when we have some distance on the issue in questions (e.g., when we are "calm" in relation to it). On the other hand, it seems more natural to operate from a first order (outside observer) perspective when we are very eager in dealing with an issue (e.g., committed to an idea for how it should be resolved) or emotionally disturbed by it (e.g., angry or mad or fearful). (p. 65)

Thus, rather than assert that one or the other set of lenses is a more useful way of thinking about our clinical practice, we consider each lens as essential to bifocal vision and that this quality of depth perception is necessary for efficacious clinical practice. Rather than promoting one set of thought rules as the more appropriate one, we consider our tasks that of helping each student discover the various ways she or he has of seeing differently.

Endnote

After Auerswald (1985, 1987), we use the term *epistemology* to denote the set of rules used by a specific group of people (e.g., family counselors or therapists) to define social "reality" (i.e., "what we cannot wish away" Berger & Luckmann, 1966); *paradigm* to denote a set of rules that define a subunit of reality; *theory* to denote an idea or a set of ideas that actually or potentially contribute to a paradigm; and *map* or *model* to denote a concrete, metaphorical specification of an epistemology, a paradigm, or a theory.

References

Amatea, E., & Sherrard, P. (1994), The ecosystemic view: A choice of lenses. *Journal of Mental Health Counseling, 16*, 6–21.

Andersen, T. (1987). The reflecting team: Dialogue and meta-dialogue in clinical work. *Family Process, 26*, 415–428.

Andersen, T. (Ed.). (1991) . *The reflecting team: Dialogues and dialogues about dialogues.* New York: Norton.

Auerswald, E. H. (1985). Thinking about thinking in family therapy. *Family Process, 24*, 1–12.

Auerswald, E. H. (1987). Epistemological confusion in family therapy and research. *Family Process, 26*, 317–330.

Bateson, G. (1977). The thing of it is. In M. Katz, W. Marsh, & G. Thompson (Eds.), *Explorations of planetary culture at the Lindisfarne conferences: Earth's answer* (pp. 142–155). New York: Harper & Row.

Bateson, G. (1979). *Mind and nature: A necessary unity.* New York: E. P. Dutton.

Bateson, M. C. (1977). Daddy, can a scientist be wise? In J. Brockman (Ed.), *About Bateson* (pp. 57–74). New York: E. P. Dutton.

Berger, M., & Dammann, C. (1982). Live supervision as context, treatment and training. *Family Process, 21*, 337–344.

Berger, P., & Luckmann, T. (1966). *The social construction of reality.* Garden City, NY: Doubleday.

Brand, S. (1976). For god's sake, Margaret: Conversation with Gregory Bateson and Margaret Mead. *The Co-Evolution Quarterly, 10*, 32–44.

Colby, A., & Damon, W. (1992) *Some do care: Contemporary lives of moral commitment.* New York: Free Press.

Coser, L. (1956). *The functions of social conflict.* New York: Free Press.

Dewey, J., & Bentley, A. (1973). The knowing and the known. In R. Handy & E. C. Harwood (Eds.), *Useful procedures of inquiry* (pp. 89–190). Great Barrington, MA: Behavior Research Council. (Original work published 1949)

Held, B., & Pols, B. (1985). The confusion about epistemology and "epistemology" and what to do about it. *Family Process, 24*, 509–516.

Howard, G. (1991). Cultural tales: A narrative approach to thinking, cross-cultural psychology, and psychotherapy. *American Psychologist, 46*, 187–197.

Huber, C. H. (1994). *Ethical, legal, and professional issues in the practice of marriage and family therapy* (2nd ed.). New York: Merrill.

Hunt, M. (1990). *The compassionate beast.* New York: Morrow.

Keeney, B. (1982). What is an epistemology of family therapy? *Family Process, 21*, 153–168.

Keeney, B. (1983). *Aesthetics of change.* New York: Guilford.

Kidder, R. M. (1995). *How good people make tough choices.* New York: Morrow.

Kitchener, K. S. (1984). Intuition, critical evaluation, and ethical principles: The foundation for ethical decisions in counseling psychology. *Counseling Psychologist, 12*, 43–55.

Kitchener, K. S. (1986). Teaching applied ethics in counselor education: An integration of psychological processes and philosophical analysis. *Journal of Counseling and Development, 64*, 306–310.

Kolb, D. A. (1984). *Experiential learning.* Englewood Cliffs, NJ: Prentice Hall.

Krueger-Casper, C. (1995). *Mystic, Irishman, radical, theologian, partner, friend.* Unpublished manuscript.

Loder, J. E. (1989). *The transforming moment.* Colorado Springs, CO: Helmers & Howard.

Mair, M. (1988). Psychology as storytelling. *International Journal of Construct Psychology, 1*, 125–137.

McNamee, S., & Gergen, K. J. (Eds.). (1992). *Therapy as social construction.* Newbury Park, CA: Sage.

Moyers, W. (Producer), & Grubin, D. (Director). (1994). *Facing evil* [Film]. (Available from Films for the Humanities and Sciences, P. O. Box 2053, Princeton, NJ 08543)

Neill, J. R., & Kniskern, D. P. (Eds.). (1982). *From psyche to system: The evolving therapy of Carl Whitaker.* New York: Guilford.

Papajohn, J., & Speigel, J. (1975). *Transactions in families.* San Francisco, CA: Jossey Bass.

Papp, P. (1980). Greek chorus and other techniques of paradoxical therapy. *Family Process, 19*, 45–57.

Parry, A., & Doan, R. (1994). *Story re-visions: Narrative therapy in a postmodern world.* New York: Guilford.

Piercy, F., Sprenkle, D., & Constantine, L. (1986). Family members' perceptions of live observation/supervision. *Contemporary Family Therapy, 8(3)*, 332–342.

Politano, K. (1995). *My personal hall of fame.* Unpublished manuscript.

Rokeach, M. (1973). *The nature of human values.* New York: Free Press.

Satir, V. (1972). *Peoplemaking.* Palo Alto, CA: Science and Behavior Books.

Senge, P. M. (1990). *The fifth discipline.* New York: Doubleday.

Senge, P. M. , Roberts, C., Ross, R., Smith, B., & Kleiner, A. (1994). *The fifth discipline fieldbook.* New York: Doubleday.

Sennett, R. (1970). *The uses of disorder.* New York: Knopf.

Sherrard, P.A.D., Lord, L.S., Lord, S. L., & Pritchard, S. T. (1991, Winter). Cybernetics and ethics: Steering through the dilemmas of professional practice. *IAMFC Newsletter*, 1–2.

Sherry, P., Teschendorf, R., Anderson, S., & Guzman, F. (1991). Ethical beliefs and behaviors of college counseling center professionals. *Journal of College Student Development, 32*, 350–358.

Smith, J., Smith, T., & Salts, C. (1991). Effects of supervisory interruptions on therapists and clients. *American Journal of Family Therapy, 19(3)*, 23–31.

Speigel, J. (1971). *Transactions.* New York: Science House.

White, M., & Epston, D. (1992). *Literate means to therapeutic ends.* New York: Norton.

Wiener, N. (1948). *Cybernetics.* Cambridge, MA: Technology Press.

Young, T. (1989–1990). A critical look at the one-way screen. *Dulwich Center Newsletter*, 64-70.

Zohar, A. (1990). *The quantum self.* New York: Quill/William Morrow.

■ ■ ■

PART IV

EPILOGUE

8

Epilogue: Social Constructionism in the Evolution of Family Therapy

Karl Tomm, MD

The chapters in this monograph point toward some important growing edges in the field of couple and family therapy. They describe contemporary innovations in narrative, collaborative language systems and solution-focused work. The therapeutic practices of externalizing (White & Epston, 1990), restorying (White & Epston, 1990), not knowing (Anderson & Goolishian, 1992), reflecting (Andersen, 1991), and attending to exceptions (de Shazer, 1985) are extending our possibilities as clinicians. The different approaches to therapy reported here hold a great deal in common. Not only are they pushing the limits of the field, they are all supported by the insights of social constructionism. Thus, I concur with Shelley Boughner, A. Spencer Davis, and Grace Ann Mims (Chapter 1) about the potential for social construction theory to provide a foundation for family work as we enter the 21st century.

Social constructionism allows for a multiplicity of perspectives and a methodology of discourse that fosters multiple descriptions and alternative explanations of human experience. It offers a dialogic means to mediate contradictions and to co-construct solutions. It opens interventive possibilities that are often unthinkable for clinicians immersed in modernist assumptions and empirical methods. With the emergence of social constructionism, there have been shifts in such notions as the self, relationships, context, and responsibility. With respect to the self, social constructionists emphasize the view that our sense of self is generated through the conversations about ourselves in which we are embedded. Relationships are not just the passive outcome of interaction but a proactive process of co-construction depending on how each interactant gives meaning to the events and behaviors taking place. The social constructionist perspective also shifts the notion of context from one of constraint and limitation to one of opportunity to co-create possibilities for giving voice to one's own views or those of others. There is also a shift in the notion of responsibility from individual culpability and blame to relational responsibility, where there is a realization of how we collectively co-construct the meanings that provide the basis for individual action. I suspect that many of our basic ideas about human beings and about relationships among them will eventually be reformulated as a result of social construction theory. These possibilities are very exciting.

The connection between social constructionism and family therapy is still very recent for many therapists. Given the current ascendency of social construction theory in relation to therapy, it might be useful to reflect on how family therapy became connected to social constructionism. I can still remember the moment a few years ago when I first realized that I was, in effect, a practicing social constructionist. It was a realization that dawned on me after a series of changes in how I thought about my work as a clinician.

There are many perspectives and stories about how family therapy has evolved and how the social constructionist perspective became so relevant. What follows is my own personal view and is based on my reality as a White, middle-class, heterosexual male who has spent his whole career in an academic setting in Canada. In many respects, my professional development seems to have followed some of the major innovations and changes in the field of family therapy during the past 30 years. I will take advantage of this connection to offer a personalized account of some major developments in the field that are grounded in my particular experiences. In the process I hope to indicate how social constructionism is relevant and what some of its difficulties or limitations might be.

When I undertook professional training in the early 1960s as a medical student and as a psychiatric resident, I was schooled in the empirical tradition of modernist medical science. I was taught to be objective and precise in my observations of human behavior. I was a conscientious student and tried to be as rigorous as possible in diagnosing and treating patients. The people I was working with were referred to as patients then, not as persons, clients, customers, or commission-givers. The designation by health care providers of a person as a *patient* reflects a powerful political action. It discloses a rigid hierarchy within the health care system with professionals on top and patients on the bottom. The dominance of professionals is coupled with a submissiveness among patients whose sense of self-control and autonomy is severely compromised by the decisions made by the professionals. I was not aware of the pathologizing effects of this hierarchy during the early years of my career, yet I actively participated in creating them. I simply accepted the social status offered to me, the doctor, and saw myself as a professional with expert knowledge. Accordingly, I expected my patients to defer to my "superior" knowledge and skills. In so doing, I inadvertently deskilled my patients and invited them to become dependent on me. I was entirely oblivious at that time to my part in the social construction of professional privilege and patient vulnerability.

The mental disorders I diagnosed then were assumed to exist within individuals who then became the focus of my interventions in treatment. This objectivist and individualist orientation is still dominant in the mental health field today and currently is being promoted by the *Diagnostic and Statistical Manual of Mental Disorders* (4th ed.; *DSM–IV*) of the American Psychiatric Association (1994). I was trained to accept the authority of the *DSM* during those early years, but I have since come to regard it as one of the major pathologizing documents in our culture (Tomm, 1990).

My student views began to change in 1968, when I first became interested in family relationships as an important influence on the behavior and mental well-being of individuals. The original triggering event was a clinical experience I had with a 14-year-old adolescent who was admitted to my ward because she kept running away from home. I became curious about what she was running away from and asked to see her family. When her parents and younger brother came in, I found all three of them to be deeply concerned and extremely caring. Why would she be running away from such nice people? This confused me and for a while I was completely bewildered. My curiosity grew and, along with it, my fascination with why family members did what they did. Nathan Epstein happened to pass through Vancouver about that time and gave a tantalizing lecture on family therapy. I was so impressed that I decided to join his program at McMaster University in Hamilton, Ontario, Canada.

At McMaster I was introduced to Ludwig von Bertalanffy's general systems theory (1968) as a framework for understanding families as whole systems. I recall struggling for some time to understand the systems theory truism that "the whole is more than the sum of the parts." The statement made sense intuitively, but just exactly what did it mean? It wasn't until it became apparent to me that it was the unique relationships between the component parts, which existed in addition to the parts and made the whole more than the sum, that I finally understood. This insight about the centrality of relationships was the key that made it possible for me to begin making a genuine shift from thinking in terms of individual persons to thinking in terms of family systems. Subsequently, I became interested in Gregory Bateson's work (1971) about the reciprocal nature of relationships and tried to understand the interaction between family members in terms of cybernetic feedback loops. I even developed a concrete model of circular pattern diagramming by applying the cybernetic metaphor to conduct a systems oriented clinical assessment (Tomm, 1980). I assumed that the better I understood the patterns of recurrent interaction between the members of a family, the more systemic I became in my assessment. Although I succeeded in adopting a systems perspective back then, I remained an empirical observer and continued to locate myself outside the system. I simply shifted from describing "observed persons" to describing "observed family systems."

In the late 1970s, I became more sensitive to the fact that it was family members' constructions of meaning regarding their life situations that were significant in determining their actions and interaction patterns. Once again it was a clinical experience that triggered a shift in me. A man with whom I had worked in individual, couple, and family therapy committed suicide. He was in a very difficult life situation but I was still shocked. I felt that my work with him had been a failure (Tomm, 1985). My confidence in my professional knowledge and skills was shaken to the core. I began to question everything I knew and consequently opened myself to a deeper kind of learning. I was ready to learn from colleagues who were radically different from me in their ways of thinking and practicing.

During a subsequent sabbatical in Europe during 1978–1979, I came across the work of the Milan team in Italy. I found their book, *Paradox and Counterparadox* (Selvini Palazzoli, Boscolo, Cecchin, & Prata, 1978), confusing and read it three times before I began to understand. Luigi Boscolo and Gianfranco Cecchin, the two male members of the Milan team, eventually became mentors for me during this phase of my professional development. I was especially intrigued by their method of asking circular questions. The family's answers to these questions were used to generate functional explanations, where it was assumed that the beliefs that families constructed about their situation determined the problematic patterns of family interaction which served some function for the system. For instance, if a certain behavior was considered bad or crazy the patterns of interaction around that behavior became very negative and critical. This negativity, of course, simply served to maintain the problem which in turn could serve a function, for instance of distracting the family from other more serious problems. Redefining the presenting problem with a positive connotation in therapy challenged the negative beliefs and could lead to a very different pattern of interaction, perhaps allowing the other problems to be addressed. The therapeutic task became one of creating a positive connotation that might enable a change in the family's meanings or beliefs.

In adopting the Milan approach, I began an ideological shift from being an empiricist to becoming a constructivist. This was not easy for me and took some time. In the process I took some theoretical guidance from Vern Cronen and Barnett Pearce's communications theory (1980) and Ernst von Glasersfeld's radical constructivism (1984). I shifted from thinking in terms of "first order observed systems" to trying to grasp the notion of "second order observing systems." I was interested in what family members saw and believed and how their patterns of seeing and believing influenced their interaction with each other. I was also interested in what my professional colleagues and I saw and believed that influenced our interaction with the family. Given that I, as a therapist, was making observations that were influencing me and my behavior, I too was part of the system of therapeutic concern. Changes in how situations and behaviors were construed and given meaning were often called for in the therapeutic system as well as in the family system. This shift to a second order perspective, to look at my looking to see what I was seeing and to listen to my listening to hear what I was hearing, constituted a major transformation in my patterns of thinking as a therapist. For the first time I could see how certain family members' views of one member as "sick" and how my own professional views of that person as "the patient" reinforced other family members, pejorative views and was so pathologizing of that person. Recognizing these pathologizing effects led to a search for different ways of looking, for ways to see persons that could have healing effects instead. The focus became one of searching for constructs or construals that were positive and enabling of views that supported the health of families and their members.

For several years, I felt quite comfortable with constructivism as a theoretical basis for this second order perspective. But gradually I came to recognize some of the inconsistencies between my constructivist theory and my methods of practice. For instance, during clinical conversations I found myself engaged in actively co-constructing new meanings together with clients and their families. The primary locus for a change in meaning appeared to be in the therapeutic conversation that was taking place. Any changes in cognitive constructs held by individuals seemed to come later. In other words, the change was initially interpersonal and secondarily intrapersonal. Humberto Maturana's theory of knowledge (Maturana & Varela, 1987) helped me appreciate more fully how social interaction was the source of meaning. His explanation of languaging as the "consensual coordination of the consensual coordination of action" placed language squarely in the social domain and enabled me to move further into the interpersonal space. Later when I heard about Ken Gergen's (1991) work I realized that I had not been a constructivist at all. I was actually a practicing social constructionist! In both my thinking and my practice I already had been giving priority to the interaction between family members and between them and myself as the source of new meanings. Not only were we coordinating our interaction, we were co-constructing meaning and awareness about how these meanings and awarenesses influenced patterns of interaction and relationship. Thus, my immersion into the Milan approach was my first explicit experience of applied social constructionism.

Of the therapeutic approaches described in this book, I am most familiar with narrative work. The approaches illustrate three major developments in applied social constructionism that have come into prominence after the Milan approach emerged. In my view they all reflect variations within the second order perspective of observing systems. When I first became involved with Michael White during the mid-1980s, I was drawn to his method of asking questions that externalized problems by separating them from persons. I had already developed my own method of asking reflexive questions (Tomm, 1987) and immediately recognized the liberating effect of externalizing questions in releasing people from the constraining effects of socially constructed descriptions of themselves and their relationships. In this externalizing work, the therapist adopts the perspective of seeing clients and families as trapped in family views or cultural views that are pathologizing. The therapist's perspective orients him or her to engage in conversations that open space for clients to see themselves as oppressed by the views that contribute to a negative identity. Once clients see themselves in this way they automatically become oriented toward escaping the oppression of such pathologizing descriptions. Later, Michael, together with his colleague David Epston, began to focus on methods to reauthor the stories of a person's life as a means to actively co-construct an alternative identity that was healthier. As a result, the so-called narrative approach was born (White & Epston, 1990). With narrative therapy, clients become empowered to protest their oppression and to selectively embrace alternative accounts of themselves and their relationships that support wellness. The interview itself becomes a process of socially co-constructing preferred narrative identities. I have found narrative methods extremely helpful in my clinical work and continue to use them on a regular basis.

Though I personally have not been very deeply immersed in solution-focused or collaborative language systems approaches, I see them as also using the interview process to co-construct preferred realities. Collaborative language systems therapy with its emphasis on "not knowing" appears to privilege a social deconstruction process by questioning the certainty inherent in the family's prevailing views. Implicitly, other less constraining views are afforded more space. The genuine curiosity behind the questions also invites clients to become more aware of additional knowledge they have available as potential resources for themselves. The solution-focused approach, on the other hand, privileges a shift in attention away from problems to client resources and competencies that constitute *exceptions* to the problem. The therapist selectively guides the client to notice these exceptions and also to become selective in what he or she sees which can become the basis for a reconstruction of the client's experience of self and a basis for a different course of action. All of these recent approaches clearly depend on the assumption that the social process of a therapeutic conversation can be used to co-construct realities of competence and "wellness," instead of diagnostic deficits and mental "illness."

Over the past few years I have felt another qualitatively different kind of shift gathering momentum in the field. This has been the increasing attention to the politics involved in the social construction of the realities that organize people's lives. In the past, the political process involved in therapy has tended to remain implicit and covert. But now, with a growing awareness of the feasibility of constructing alternative meanings for any experience or situation, along with an awareness that each meaning has different consequences, the issue of which meaning is chosen to be selected out and given priority over others is coming into the foreground as of paramount importance. Which construal or "reality" gets selected to be acted upon? Who decides which construct and what meaning is to be privileged? What are the immediate and remote effects of adopting one construction as opposed to another? Who is liable to be advantaged or disadvantaged by these effects? Do the various stakeholders (client, therapist, and multiple third parties) have equal say in privileging one construction over others? If not, why not? To what extent are we aware of our own power as therapists to bring forth the constructs that we prefer? And what constructions do we need as therapists to adjudicate ethically among alternative constructions and still remain consistent with our therapeutic intentions to help clients? These questions have led to increased disclosure and acknowledgement of the political process involved in the construction of social realities. The field of family therapy is now beginning to grapple publicly with these political issues.

The first major area in which these politics were exposed with a substantial amount of energy was in the domain of gender. Feminist family therapists began to point out the ways in which male constructions were often being systematically privileged and how this usually disadvantaged females, not only in families but also among therapists (Goldner, 1985; Hare-Mustin, 1987; MacKinnon & Miller, 1987). The field of family therapy started to pay attention to the knowledge that was available through the feminist movement. My late partner, Winnie Tomm, was a major contributor to my own understanding of the pervasive injustices in families and cultures that are based on gendered assumptions about reality. She was a philosopher who became a feminist scholar (W. Tomm & Hamilton, 1988; W. Tomm, 1989, 1995) and helped me experientially as well as intellectually to open up some significant blind spots in my male-based reality. Once my awareness began to grow and we worked through some changes toward more gender equity in our own relationship by liberating ourselves from some cultural stereotypes, I was more effective in enabling this process with the couples I saw in therapy.

The second major area in which a palpable awareness of the politics of the social construction of reality emerged for me was in racism and ethnocentrism. The Just Therapy team in New Zealand including Kiwi Tamasese, Charles Waldegrave, Wally Campbell, and Flora Tuhaka and the Peoples Institute for Survival and Beyond in New Orleans helped me begin to see the pervasiveness of White European domination of other cultures through overt and covert colonization (Chisom & Washington, 1996; Tamasese & Waldegrave, 1993). White European values have been socially constructed as superior to anything else, which has served to justify all kinds of exploitation and oppression. The Just Therapy group not only draws attention to these injustices but they also develop methods to address the power imbalances through caucusing and accountability structures (Tamasese & Waldegrave, 1993). They self-consciously create a process in which a dominant or privileged group is invited to hear and acknowledge the experiences and constructions of the marginalized or disadvantaged group. This privileging of marginalized voices is carried out to the extent that collective efforts to rectify the imbalance of power are eventually undertaken. Furthermore, the dominant group remains accountable to the marginalized group. For instance, when a male therapist works with a female client, he remains accountable to the women in the treatment center for his work with her. Similarly, when a White therapist works with a Maori family, he or she remains accountable to the Maori staff and a group of Maori elders for his or her clinical work with that family. This deliberate realignment of the historical hierarchy serves to diminish the probability of continuing patterns of colonization, exploitation, and oppression. Similar accountability structures could conceivably be constructed to counter the pathologizing prejudices of heterosexism, classism, professionalism, and parentism as well. In my opinion, family therapy has only scratched the surface in attending to these larger social issues.

Why do I consider social justice so important in the development of family therapy? There is a virtual epidemic of sexism, heterosexism, racism, ethnocentrism, classism, parentism, professionalism, and so forth in our culture and communities. It is an epidemic that continues to generate an enormous amount of conflict and misery within and between individuals and families. An epidemic cannot be contained by treating the "illness" in single cases alone. The source of the epidemic needs to be addressed. The need for the social construction of more justice at all levels is becoming more and more apparent. When I look to see how our culture is creating and replicating structures of social injustice that generate pathologizing dynamics between us and within us as human beings, I feel compelled ethically to do something about altering our cultural drift as well as doing therapy. My growing awareness of these conditions is making it increasingly difficult to remain in my comfortable office and help families "adapt" to pathologies in the culture outside. Ironically, as a clinician I am benefiting financially from these cultural pathologies. I am pleased that I am becoming more and more uncomfortable with my professional privilege and am looking for ways to intervene in the social domain as well as with families in therapy.

The Just Therapy group is providing some important leadership in addressing larger social issues like poverty as well as doing therapy. With respect to the clinical approaches described in this volume, issues of social justice are being addressed much more fully in narrative work than in collaborative language systems and solution-focused work. However, the narrative metaphor itself may inadvertently be restraining further movement in this direction. The term *narrative* points to a story and implicitly privileges the storyline or text of the story. It is too easy to lose sight of the politics involved and the social injustice when looking at and listening to stories. I believe we need some new metaphors to help us fulfill the potential of these most recent developments in the field to address the larger political dynamics in our cultures that are so pathologizing of persons, families, and friendships. I do not know what these new metaphors might be. At this point, I am only trying to draw attention to what I see as some possibilities in the future.

Thus, as I see it, there have been three major phases in the development of the family therapy field so far. To propose three phases like this is of course a social construction in itself. I do so being mindful of the possible consequences of offering this particular construction of our history. Although there has probably always been overlap among these developments, I describe them as if they were sequential to suggest an overall direction in our collective movement. The directionality implies some inevitability in the initiatives toward what I value and prefer.

To recapitulate briefly, the first phase was a shift from looking at separate individuals to looking at individuals as parts of family systems. During this phase there was an emphasis on viewing families as mechanistic systems where family relationships were based on reactions to one another that were regulated by rules and homeostatic dynamics to maintain family patterns. Some of the negative consequences of this perspective were to trivialize both persons and families and to justify the authority of professionals to act on them unilaterally. The second phase was a shift from first order (observed) systems to second order (observing) systems, that is, from looking at families as systems of persons interacting to looking at their looking to see what they were seeing. We began to look at families as observing systems who, through their observing of one another and their patterns of interaction, gave meaning to events, and these meanings in turn organized their responses to one another. This shift in theory was accompanied by a shift in practice from trying to alter interactional behaviors directly to altering the meanings attributed to those behaviors. Most of the innovations described in this book focus on elaborating methods for achieving this. Part of the second phase entailed looking at our own looking as professionals to see what we were seeing and how that seeing organized us. It was this aspect of the second phase that ushered in the third phase, which is currently underway. It has to do with looking at and listening to the cultural, community, and family politics of looking and listening, including our own looking and listening. It is a shift from simply looking at the family's looking at one another that organizes their actions (and looking at our own looking that organizes us in our actions) to looking at the real political effects of certain patterns of seeing that orient and influence our patterns of behavior. The third phase entails giving full consideration to the power dynamics that follow from how we and others see things.

Social constructionism is an extremely valuable resource in supporting an expansion of the second phase of family therapy because it provides a means for generating alternative realities. However, I am not convinced that it alone can adequately support the third phase. The reason for this is that there is no clear basis within the theory to select and act on one possible reality rather than another. Furthermore, social constructionism does not explain how the social systems that construct various realities came into existence to start with. The most it can claim is that we as human beings interact to construct the reality that we exist and that we do construct realities. In effect, the theory pulls itself up with its own bootstraps and remains groundless. It is this groundlessness of social constructionism that limits its acceptability for many theoreticians and clinicians, especially those who are looking for a basis for making choices among various realities. In other words, the strength of social constructionism in making alternative realities possible is also its weakness.

In my opinion, the third phase in the evolution of family therapy requires a theory or a belief that provides a basis for ethical choices among alternative realities. To make a choice is to take a political stand. Even if we choose to not make a choice, we implicitly support the prevailing power structures. Social constructionism has been successful in making it possible for us to see more alternatives and to become conscious of the choices available to us. It brings us to a point of reflection where we can look at our looking to see multiple possibilities, but it does not take us through the next step of choosing among them. It can help me raise the question, "Am I going to choose to see things in ways that allow me to live with and perhaps even support the status quo, or am I going to choose to see things in ways that compel me to take some action for change?" But it does not help me answer this question. It does not help me in actually making a choice. This is a major limitation.

Social constructionism does not espouse specific values like love, respect, and justice. Indeed, social construction theory can be used for negative purposes. The awareness that realities can be socially constructed has led to the deliberate construction of hatred for war, oppression for colonization, exploitation for accumulated wealth, and hedonism for immediate gratification. The advertising community certainly knows about the self-serving effects of constructing consumer need to sell a product. In our present culture, there is an insidious process of an increasing commodification of persons, relationships, and even meanings. This places us at risk for giving even more priority to entrepreneurial values over humanistic values. For instance, it appears that managed care companies are actively exploiting human love to maximize the "bottom line" of profit. Thus, there are some real dangers in the power of the social construction theory. Given its emphasis on here-and-now social interaction, it also risks the danger of abandoning the constructive influences of cultural traditions and heritages. In these respects social constructionism remains vulnerable to cynicism and spiritual bankruptcy.

So what could I use to answer the question about which construct, idea, explanation, or perspective to select out and favor? Should I return to some form of objectivity to adjudicate the relative truth of any particular view? Should I draw upon the knowledges available in political theory and moral philosophy? Should I draw upon the wisdom of various cultural traditions to identify preferred views? Should I draw upon the values of various world religions and exercise faith to guide my choices? Or should I support personal spiritual experience as a basis for ethical knowledge?

Among these alternatives, I am most attracted to finding a resource in a rich spiritual life for making ethical choices. Unfortunately, I remain rather limited in my spiritual development (as a result of deliberate inattention to this aspect of my life following a decision I took in my youth to reject anything remotely associated with organized religion) and need to find help elsewhere. My schooling predisposed me to favor frameworks that are logical and scientific. As noted earlier, this disposition became well developed during my medical and psychiatric training. However, it ultimately left me with a serious dilemma during my early career when I recognized the limitations of the objectivist perspective. Fortunately, I came across Maturana's theory of knowledge with which I could resonate (Maturana & Varela, 1980, 1987). It is grounded in a scientific biology yet does not depend on objectivity. Indeed, Maturana had to eschew objectivity to explain how "the observer" arose to make scientific observations. He offers a refreshing second order perspective on science, one that includes the observer in what is observed.

What has been of particular interest to me in Maturana's theory is that he discloses the centrality of love in the evolution of multicellular living systems as well as in the evolution of human relationships and culture. He points out how we exist as a result of a gigantic phylogenetic and ontogenic drift in which love has been a core generative process. Maturana also recognizes the fundamental importance of language and its social origins in bringing forth specific distinctions in our consensual coordination of action with one another. In this respect his work is consistent with social constructionism. He goes further, however, and emphasizes that love is what enabled the intensity of recurrent social interaction that was required for language to arise in the first place. It follows that love might be the most appropriate foundation for any therapy and for any social action for change. I have adopted this assumption. It gives me a basis for making choices in the politics of the third phase. Keeping in mind Maturana's descriptions of love as "acknowledging the legitimacy of the other in relation to the self" and "opening space for the existence of the other," I open myself to see the conditions and hear the experiences of others and to act on their behalf as well as my own. I can orient myself to choose those constructs and actions that bring forth more love in whatever situation I am working. Thus, I see myself as using social constructionism within the context of Maturana's *bringforthism*, because the latter offers me a rationale for ethical decision making. Whether I personally will continue to privilege these frames of reference into the 21st century or not remains to be seen.

References

American Psychiatric Association. (1994). *Diagnostic and statistical manual of mental disorders* (4th ed.). Washington, DC: Author.

Andersen, T. (Ed.). (1991). *The reflecting team: Dialogues and dialogues about the dialogues.* New York: Norton.

Anderson, H., & Goolishian, H. (1992). The client is the expert: A not-knowing approach to therapy. In S. McNamee & K. Gergen (Eds.), *Therapy as social construction* (pp. 25–39). Newbury Park, CA: Sage.

Bateson, G. (1971). *Steps to an ecology of mind.* New York: Ballantine.

Chisom, R., & Washington, M. (1996). *Undoing racism: A philosophy of international social change.* New Orleans, LA: The People's Institute for Survival and Beyond.

Cronen, V., & Pearce, B. (1980). *Communication, action, and meaning: The creation of social realities.* New York: Praeger.

de Shazer, S. (1985). *Keys to solution in brief therapy.* New York: Norton.

Gergen, K. (1991). *The saturated self: Dilemmas of identity in contemporary life.* Glenview, IL: Basic Books.

Goldner, V. (1985). Feminism and family therapy. *Family Process, 24*, 31–47.

Hare-Mustin, R. (1987). The problem of gender in family therapy theory. *Family Process, 26*, 15–27.

MacKinnon, L., & Miller, D. (1987). The new epistemology and the Milan approach: Feminist and sociopolitical considerations. *The Journal of Marital and Family Therapy, 13*, 139–155.

Maturana, H. R., & Varela, F. (1980). *Autopoiesis and cognition* (Vol. 42). Boston: D. Reidel.

Maturana, H. R., & Varela, F. (1987). *The tree of knowledge: The biological roots of human understanding.* Boston: Shambhala.

Selvini Palazzoli, M., Boscolo, L., Cecchin, G., & Prata, G. (1978). *Paradox and counterparadox: A new model in the therapy of the family in schizophrenic transition.* New York: Jason Aronson.

Tamasese, K., & Waldegrave, C. (1993). Cultural and gender accountability and the Just Therapy approach. *Journal of Feminist Family Therapy, 5*, 29–45.

Tomm, K. (1980). Towards a cybernetic systems approach to family therapy at the University of Calgary. In D.S. Freeman (Ed.), *Perspectives on family therapy* (pp. 3–18). Toronto: Butterworths Press.

Tomm, K. (1985). Struggling with the threat of suicide. In S. Coleman (Ed.), *Failures in family therapy* (pp. 300–329). New York: Guilford Press.

Tomm, K. (1987). Interventive interviewing: Part II reflexive questioning as a means to enable self healing. *Family Process, 26*, 153–185.

Tomm, K. (1990). A critique of the DSM. *Dulwich Centre Newsletter, 3*, 5–8.

Tomm, W. (1995). *Bodied mindfulness: Women's spirits, bodies, and places.* Waterloo, Ontario: Wilfred Laurier University Press.

Tomm, W. (Ed.). (1989). *The effects of feminist approaches on research methodologies*. Waterloo, Ontario: Wilfred Laurier University Press.

Tomm, W., & Hamilton, G. (Eds.). (1988). *Gender bias in scholarship: The pervasive prejudice*. Waterloo, Ontario: Wilfred Laurier University Press

von Bertalanffy, L. (1968). *General system theory*. New York: George Braziller.

von Glasersfeld, E. (1984). An introduction to radical constructivism. In P. Watzlawick (Ed.), *The invented reality* (pp. 17–40). New York: Norton.

White, M., & Epston, D. (1990). *Narrative means to therapeutic ends*. New York: Norton.

■ ■ ■